LIMITED GOVERNMENT

PRENTICE-HALL
CONTEMPORARY COMPARATIVE POLITICS SERIES
JOSEPH LaPALOMBARA, Editor

published

forthcoming

CARL J. FRIEDRICH

Harvard University

Prentice-Hall, Inc.,
Englewood Cliffs, N. J.

LIMITED GOVERNMENT:
A COMPARISON

Library of Congress Cataloging in Publication Data

Friedrich, Carl Joachim, 1901–
    Limited government: a comparison.

    (Prentice-Hall contemporary comparative politics
series)
    Bibliography: p. 129
    1. Constitutional history.   2. Comparative
government.   I. Title.
JF51.F723   320.3   74-802
ISBN   0-13-537167-8
ISBN   0-13-537159-7 (pbk.)

LIMITED GOVERNMENT: A COMPARISON
Carl J. Friedrich

Printed in the United States of America

10 9 8 7 6 5 4 3 2 1

PRENTICE-HALL INTERNATIONAL, INC., London
PRENTICE-HALL OF AUSTRALIA, PTY. LTD., Sydney
PRENTICE-HALL OF CANADA, LTD., Toronto
PRENTICE-HALL OF INDIA PRIVATE LIMITED, New Delhi
PRENTICE-HALL OF JAPAN, INC., Tokyo

to the loving memory of my mother
Charlotte Friedrich
1868–1973

CONTENTS

FOREWORD

The organization of the Contemporary Comparative Politics Series is based on a number of assumptions and guidelines that are worth calling to the reader's attention. Foremost among these is that the undergraduate student of comparative politics is less interested in political science than we might hope, but more capable of synthetic analysis than we may imagine. If this is so, then it would be an enormous mistake to pretend to organize an introductory series around one or more half-baked "theories" of politics or political systems—theories that are difficult for even the more hardened members of the profession to digest. It would seem equally debatable whether the undergraduate student has a strong desire to learn in depth the institutional arrangements and workings of any single political system, whether that system be as established as that of Great Britain or as new and exotic as that of Tanzania.

What, then, can we expect of those undergraduates who study comparative politics? First, I think that they are quickly turned off by simplistic or spurious efforts to lend the discipline a theoretical elegance it manifestly does not possess; second, that saturation treatments of single political systems are as unpalatable today when the countries are individually packaged as they were when several countries appeared between the same hard covers; third, that the undergraduates sitting in our classrooms might very well be turned on if they learned what sorts of things political scientists do and what kinds of knowledge of the political process they can glean from the things we do. These things, incidentally, would involve not merely data-gathering on some aspect of the political system, but also speculative and normative considerations about the relationship between politics and the good life. We can expect that if the things to be written and lectured about are carefully chosen and intelligently organized, the undergraduate will display a striking capacity to synthesize information and to develop skills in analyzing political phenomena that are at least as impressive as, say, those of a New York taxi driver, a voluble parent, or a political orator.

Another major assumption underlying the organization of the series is that the topics included should not reflect a commitment to an institutional or behavioral, normative or empirical approach. If members of the profession are still battling about such things, let them spare undergraduates the arid, scholastic, and essentially unproductive nature of such encounters. The authors of this series are neither bare-facts empiricists nor "cloud-ninety" political moralists; they neither sanctify nor abominate institutional or behavioral analysis, but would rather use whatever methods are available to enlighten the reader about important aspects of political life. To emphasize the important is also to be relevant, and our correlative assumption here is that the student who wants political science to be "revelant" does not mean by this that it should be banal, simple-minded, or unsystematic.

Since no series can tell us everything about politics, we have had to choose what we consider to be the important, relevant, and reasonably integrated topics. Such choices are always arbitrary to some extent. However, we have sought to accord attention to certain standard and ubiquitous institutions as well as to newer conceptual and analytical foci that have provoked a good deal of recent research and discussion. Thus the series now includes a volume on Comparative Legislatures and another on Political Corruption; it will have a volume on Comparative Legal Cultures and another on The Craft of Political Research.

In this short volume Carl J. Friedrich, one of the world's most distinguished political scientists, gives us a highly synthesized version of many of his most important ideas about politics. Drawing on a lifetime of scholarship, vast knowledge of political systems, and an unbending attachment to democratic values, Friedrich delineates for us the meaning of "constitutionalism" or limited government.

It is fitting that this volume should appear at a time when the relationship between man and his government appears universally perplexing, in democracies as well as elsewhere. Although he does not minimize the difficulties involved in efforts to keep government in the service of mankind, Friedrich makes the institutional and related conditions of democracy brilliantly clear.

Volumes to follow this one will represent what we believe is an interesting and useful mosaic that should be appealing to those who teach, those who learn about, and all of those who try to understand politics.

JOSEPH LaPALOMBARA

New Haven

LIMITED GOVERNMENT

CONSTITUTION-MAKING IN OUR TIME

1

Our time is confronted by a curious paradox in the field of constitution-making. For, on the one hand, every new nation insists that it must have a constitution if it is to be complete. On the other hand people do not have any very great confidence in the effectiveness of constitutions. People are inclined to feel that a constitution is often honored in the breach, even if they do not think that it is a mere scrap of paper, as is at times alleged by cynics.[1]

A similar paradox confronts established states with constitutions of considerable age that are no longer adequate and therefore give rise to insistent demands for constitutional reform. Such constitutional reform is now actively debated, not only in the United States, but in Canada, France, the Federal Republic of Germany, Belgium, and even traditional England and Switzerland. The problem appears to be how to alter existing constitutional arrangements in order to adapt them to new emergent conditions in the society and its politics. "Do we need a new constitution?" is a question that troubles many Americans at the present time. Recently a full-fledged new constitution has been worked out, and it has much to recommend it. Its author calls it a constitution for the American Republics; not only the federal structure, but executive-legislative relations and a good many other features of the constitution of 1787 are radically altered.[2] Nor is this the first time. Past proposals such as those of W. Y. Elliott and of Hazlitt found a strong echo. Among political scientists, there has always been a certain

[1] On this cf. Karl Löwenstein, *Political Power and the Governmental Process*, 1957, pp. 153 ff. Cf. also my *Constitutional Government and Democracy*, 1932 (4th ed., 1968).

[2] Rexford G. Tugwell, *A Model Constitution for a United Republics of America*, 1970. Already in 1938 a group of historians had discussed these matters and published *The Constitution Reconsidered*, C. Read, ed., 1938.

sentiment in favor of the British parliamentary system, as contrasted with the American presidential one, and so eminent a student and practitioner of politics as Woodrow Wilson favored the British plan.[3] Clearly many believed and still believe that constitutional structures are of great practical importance. It ill behooves so-called behavioralists to belittle institutional concern. For what are institutions but repetitive behavior? And what are constitutions but attempts to establish certain basic patterns of behavior and to limit others?

The rise of the United States to the position of a super-power has, on the other hand, misled many into overestimating the role of the American constitution and looking upon it as the key to success. Thus it has become the "in thing" for new nations. When a people becomes independent, it feels that it must have a constitution, and then often finds that it does not "work." Fortunately, the disenchantment with certain aspects of constitutionalism in older countries like the United States, Britain, and France has prevented the growth of a constitutional "myth." At the beginning of this century the American Constitution was practically a sacred document. It was an established ritual to praise the Constitution on festive occasions, especially the Fourth of July, until "Fourth of July oratory" became a term of derision to describe hollow declamatory rhetorics. Rarely was an attempt made to assess the adequacy of the Constitution. Today the situation is radically changed. Quite a few people, especially among the young, denounce the Constitution as outmoded, and as a defense of the "establishment."

Eighteenth-century legislation and constitution-making were firmly based upon the belief in reason prevalent in the age of the Enlightenment. This general outlook carried well over into the nineteenth century. The conviction of the sanctity of law can, of course, be traced back to the Middle Ages and is clearly at the center of early modern political thought. It crystallized in the formula of "a government of law and not of men."[4] Our age has lost these convictions and the corresponding preoccupations. Policy has taken the place of law as the focal point of an interest in politics. Many people nowadays believe that the important thing is to participate in the policy-making process. How such policy is then transformed into legislation is seen as a technical task, best left to lawyers, and, in many European countries, more specifically to ministries of justice. It is not surprising that this profound shift in the general outlook on law and legislation should have affected constitution-making and constitution-amending. For here, too, many imagine that what matters is agreement on policy.

---

[3] William Y. Elliott, *The Need for Constitutional Reform*, 1935; Henry Hazlitt, *A New Constitution Now*, 1942.

[4] Löwenstein, "Erscheinungsformen," *Political Power*, 1957, Chapter 4.

In that perspective, a constitutional provision appears to be a technical formula for a basic policy decision, such as, for example, "abolishing the electoral college" in the United States. But upon closer inspection it soon becomes apparent that these so-called policy decisions are vague and imprecise indications of a direction that constitutional amending is intended to take, but which have no practical significance without detailed elaboration. Thus, talk of "abolishing the electoral college," leaves many open questions, such as whether one intends to abolish, along with the college, the "federal" structure of the election of the president, with all the profound implications such a change would have for American politics. It also leaves open the question of whether American citizens not residing in an American state, such as the Puerto Ricans, should remain excluded from participating in the election of a President. The Puerto Ricans are demanding such participation, even if that amendment were not passed, thereby necessitating another amendment such as the one made for the District of Columbia. Hence, such proposals encounter fierce opposition from those whose power would be sharply reduced. Such opposition is more likely to be efficacious under democratic conditions than the support of those who would be favored by the change.

The issue of constitutionalism is further complicated by the semantic problems involved. If one believes in the "tyranny of words," or that words are just that and nothing more, one will lose faith in verbal formulations. Where the loss of faith applies to constitutions, it ultimately leads to a position I would call "manipulative indifference." Such "manipulative indifference" is succinctly expressed in Alexander Pope's well-known quip, "O'er forms of government let fools contest. That which is best administered is best." In the light of such an outlook, constitutions have largely a declaratory value. They either declare what is actually being done, or they declare what it is believed ought to be done. Both of these declarations are seen not as regulating conduct, but as expressing attitudes or wishes regarding it.[5]

Despite the widespread scepticism concerning constitutions as effective regulators of political life, many constitutions, as we said, have been adopted in the most divergent contexts since the Second World War, in France, in Italy, and in Germany, as well as in the world at large. In adopting them, not only politicians, but the public as well, have considered them regulatory devices of great significance. On reflection, even the most radical sceptic is obliged to concede that constitutional charters do mold political behavior. Most politics, most of the time, is conducted in accordance with such constitutional provisions. Where this is not so,

---

[5] Löwenstein has, in his *Political Power*, pp. 49–50, proposed the term "semantic constitution" for a constitution in which purely verbal formulas predominate.

the failure to act in accordance with them has generated strife and break-down.

One is justified in asking what is the purpose of words and phrases included in constitutions. Although it may not be fashionable to stress the purposive aspect of political phenomena, I think it is fair to say that in the eighteenth century, whatever the philosophical basis of a constitution, the significant political objective of making a constitution was freedom. Constitutionalism as a movement was directed against monarchical absolutism, with its police, its armies and wars, and its consequent oppressive restrictions upon freedom of self-expression and self-fulfillment.

It may well be doubted that freedom is the objective of constitution-makers today. The declaratory preambles of contemporary constitutions mention a variety of broad objectives, among which social justice is a recurrent theme. In view of this, it may be wise to ask what were the situations in which recent constitutions were adopted. We can consider three kinds. First, constitutionalism has been favored in countries in which totalitarian fascism had been experienced and had failed. There are, secondly, countries which have emerged from a colonial war of liberation, and, thirdly, there are federal unions calling for new forms of political cooperation, transcending state boundaries.

Let me first make just a few remarks on the third of these situations. Its most notable example is the European Community, now organized into a common market which its protagonists are seeking to escalate into a political order. Here, the main objective appears to be greater security and greater economic productivity, that is to say, an improvement in the standard of living.

The preamble of the draft constitution for the European Political Community stated that its makers were desirous, through the expansion of production, of "improving the standard of living" and "furthering the works of peace." And it added that the drafters were determined to safeguard, by their joint action, the freedom and fundamental equality of men of every condition, race, or creed. The latter formula stressed that the security objective was linked to a libertarian and egalitarian society which the constitution was intended to safeguard. But it also argued that they wished to substitute "for their historic rivalries a fusion of their essential interests by creating institutions capable of giving guidance to their future common destiny."[6] The prime purpose of the emergent constitutional order was clearly that of replacing national states with a federative international order which would necessitate detailed constitutional rules.[7]

[6] Robert R. Bowie and Carl J. Friedrich, *Studies in Federalism*, 1954, Appendix 2, p. 828.

[7] See my *Trends of Federalism in Theory and Practice*, 1968b, Chapter 2.

Turning now to the countries with totalitarian experience, the understanding of the post-totalitarian phase is complicated by a widespread assumption that the people were, in the majority, committed to totalitarianism, but then had a "change of heart." Actually, although this was the assumption of the constitution-makers, this approach was not in accordance with the facts as we now know them. The extent to which totalitarian movements had the support of the majority of the populations cannot at present be determined with any exactitude. Perhaps we shall never know what percentage of the German or Italian people supported fascism or what percentage of the French people favored the Vichy regime. Probably the percentage in all three of these cases is lower than was at one time supposed to be the case. (Around 40 percent for Germany in 1933 is the most nearly precise figure we have.)[8]

What we do know is that what these populations in fact supported is not what the movements turned out to be, but what they pretended to be. If either Mussolini or Hitler had told his people what he in fact proposed to do, namely to plunge them into war, their support would have dwindled considerably below current estimates. Furthermore, if either man had subjected himself to free elections after four years of rule, he presumably would have been defeated. What prevented these peoples from giving expression to their political views was that they had become subjects or dependents of a conquering horde of barbarians who sprang up in their own midst.[9] It was natural, therefore, that the prime objective of such postwar constitution-making should have been to avoid a recurrence of such an experience.

In a sense, this experience corresponds to that of eighteenth-century man living under absolutism. That experience had led to a radical rejection of monarchism. Since the experience of totalitarian dictatorship proved more terrible, the antagonism aroused by it was correspondingly more fanatic. From this experience arose a constitution-making sentiment, a constituent power, so to speak,[10] which was strongly determined to bar the recurrence of any such transformation of a free society into involuntary servitude. The constituent power that came into being under these conditions was determined to institutionalize freedom through a suitable constitution. Since most men realized how formidable were the potentialities of state power, they were determined to limit such state power by formal law and to provide the person with a sphere of inviolable rights.

[8] Dietrich Bracher, et al., *Die nationalsozialistische Machtergreifung*, 1960, Chapter 2, S. III–6, pp. 88 ff. and 205 ff. Cf. for this the sane and balanced estimate by Karl Löwenstein, in his *Hitler's Germany*, rev. ed., 1940, pp. 68 ff.

[9] See for this my *Totalitarian Dictatorship and Autocracy* (with Z. Brzezinski), rev. ed., 1965.

[10] Friedrich, *Constitutional Government*, pp. 131 ff.

In some ways the constellation strongly resembled that preceding the French Revolution. Freedom once more became a prime objective, modified by social justice. Remembering the extent to which fascist movements had been assisted in their rise by the use and abuse of human rights provisions they overthrew, these constitutions provided for the suspension of these rights for the parties or groups engaged in constitutional subversion. A good deal of controversy has arisen over these clauses which patently invite abuse. However, such abuse has not occurred to date, unless the outlawry of the neo-fascist or Communist parties can be considered an abuse. There is general agreement that these constitutional provisions of the so-called Bonn Constitution of the German Federal Republic have served to provide at least a part of the German people with a certain measure of political stability, and allowed the ideas associated with such constitutional democracy to take root.

By and large, post-fascist constitution-makers have not turned to the American or other successful constitutional systems for guidance.[11] Quite understandably, for example, the American Constitution's key institution, namely the Presidency, has had few advocates; the reason being that European constitution-makers felt that it was too readily pervertible into party dictatorship, the very thing these constitution-makers were most anxious to avoid. Some impact of the American constitutional system is evident in the judicial field. In both Italy and Germany, for example, a kind of constitutional court was organized which exercises a stabilizing and moderating influence.[12] However, European constitution-makers were no doubt influenced by the widespread opinion that the shortcomings of American constitutionalism were grave.[13]

The post-fascist regimes were slow to recognize the degree to which the much praised "flexibility" had contributed to the rise and takeover by the fascists. Influenced by the pro-British terminology, which contrasts a "flexible" with a "rigid" constitution,[14] it was seldom realized that another pair of adjectives might put a very different perspective on this contrast. An unstable (flexible) constitution might be contrasted with a

[11] I have called these "negative revolutions." Cf. Friedrich, *Constitutional Government*, pp. 151 ff. and the literature cited there for the several countries.

[12] Cf. Taylor Cole, "The West German Federal Constitutional Court: An Evaluation After Six Years," 1958; Gottfried Dietze, "America and Europe—Decline and Emergence of Judicial Review," 1958; Edward McWhinney, *Constitutionalism in Germany and the Federal Constitutional Court*, 1962b. Cf. also the Court's self-evaluation in *Das Bundesverfassungsgericht*.

[13] See my *The Impact of American Constitutionalism Abroad*, 1967, p. 5, and Chapter 2.

[14] Cf. also Löwenstein's masterly summary of the issue in *British Cabinet Government*, 1967a.

stable (rigid) one. Post-fascist constitution-makers, understanding this distinction, might have recognized that a stable democratic order requires separating ordinary from *constitutional* legislation and that the latter may well be much more "rigid" than the former.

That need not have prevented the elaboration of less rigid processes adapted to effective constitutional legislation needed for changing a distinctive constitutional law. A qualified majority requirement may suffice, as the experience of the German Federal Republic to date would suggest; for quite a number of significant constitutional amendments have been passed. This has happened in spite of the fact that the required qualified majority calls for effective cooperation of both major parties in the process of constitutional legislation. These amendments have occurred at quite critical periods in the evolution of the German Federal Republic.[15]

The attitude of peoples recently liberated from colonialism and imperialism is in many ways similar to that of Europeans after absolutism. There is little to be gained for the present purpose by trying to assess the relative degree of oppression and violence. In Europe such a relative degree had little to do with the kind of constitutionalism adopted. Enlightened despotism had taken some tentative steps in the direction of constitutionalism. And similarly, the more oppressive colonial systems became modified by liberalism and humanitarianism to some extent. But the basic issues remained. The argument often voiced by defenders of the colonial system, that human rights would be jeopardized by native rule, meant little to those who thought of freedom largely in terms of freedom from foreign domination.[16] Arbitrary arrest, exploitation, and poverty were an invariable feature of colonialism and imperialism. Culturally conditioned clashes over conceptions of justice often aggravated the situation.[17]

Many of the oppressed peoples felt that the development of a sound constitutional order was a later worry. Yet all of them were determined to tackle the task of building such an order. One could say that the will to create a firm framework for freedom crystallized as it had in eighteenth-century Europe. Thus a constituent power was born. However, the belief system of Western Christianity, in which the political thought of the West is embedded, was usually absent in those colonial realms. Patently, many of the communities that have adopted constitutions in this century, or who had such constitutions imposed upon them by well-intentioned colo-

---

[15] G. Leibholz and H. J. Rink, *Grundgesetz für die BRD* (hereafter cited as Leibholz, *Grundgesetz*).

[16] It is strange indeed that Isaiah Berlin, in his much quoted Inaugural, "Two Concepts of Liberty," 1958, argued that group efforts, such as national aspirations, must be understood as a search for status, rather than for freedom.

[17] A striking case of such a conflict is presented by Richard Llwellyn in his fine novel, *A Man in a Mirror*, 1961. Cf. my comments on this in *Man and His Government*, 1963b, pp. 254–255.

nial rulers, are not Christian communities. Consequently, to the extent that Western constitutionalism is part of Christian culture, the viability of constitutional orders in formerly colonial territories may well be doubted.[18] Not only human rights may be affected by the weakness of the implied belief system, but also the very central notion of the separation of powers. The problem of how to limit state power seems often much less urgent than how to employ it effectively. The developmental tasks, and not only the economic ones, are vast and pressing. Hence the question as to how to organize a government in such a way as to protect the individual in his pursuit of happiness (i.e., self-realization) loses much of its urgency. The impulse to freedom therefore gives way to other impulses that seem to require satisfaction. Usually the colonial masters had lacked a full appreciation of the distinct human values cherished by the subject people. This very fact served to frustrate effective self-expression for individuals and groups alike. As a result, a great danger was overlooked which presented itself after liberation. In the first enthusiasm of having won external freedom, native leaders were ready to deny their people full scope in helping to shape native culture and its application to politics.[19] But this, of course, does not mean that they could or would be successful constitution-makers. The widespread complaint that the new masters are out of touch with the people, or in any case unwilling to listen to public opinion, is a result of a failure to evolve viable constitutional orders.

Nothing illustrated this more dramatically than the tragedy in Nigeria. The constitution which had been developed under British aegis for this artificial entity which was compounded of antagonistic tribes could not be expected to develop effectively under the complex arrangements the Nigerians accepted as their constitution. The constitutional document[20] begins with an elaborate and nearly incomprehensible set of provisions for its own amendment. It was the result of successive attempts in 1946, 1951, and 1954 to arrive at constitutional agreement. The Nigerian story serves to demonstrate quite dramatically how doomed to failure are attempts to formalize governmental relations in terms of a constitution which rests upon a tradition of values and beliefs quite alien to the indigenous culture. No constituent group ever came into being. What has been called "tribal nationalism" by one of its native interpreters as well as other factors peculiar to Nigeria

[18] See my *Transcendent Justice*, 1964, pp. 3 ff.

[19] Lucy Mair, *Primitive Government*, 1963.

[20] Cf. Kalu Ezera, *Constitutional Developments in Nigeria*, 1960; still more formalistic is Oluwole Idowu Odumosu, *The Nigerian Constitution: History and Development*, 1963, which gives the text, pp. 309 ff. The amending provisions are found on pp. 314–16, and Professor Odumosu's comment on pp. 237 ff. Taylor Cole, in his contribution to the collection of studies he edited with Robert O. Tilman, *The Nigerian Political Scene*, 1962, also exhibited a good deal of optimism, when considered in light of later developments, although embodying cautious judgments at the time of writing.

helped to assure that Nigeria's constitution would not be a living one,[21] and hence was doomed from the start. The formidable civil war which eventually had to be fought, highlights the dangers when constitutions do not reflect the genuine culture.

Twentieth-century constitutions are invariably much more democratic than those of the eighteenth and early nineteenth centuries. Even the facade constitutions of the peoples' democracies [22] insist upon this label. For true constitutions in the Western sense a very perplexing problem is hidden here. If democracy is interpreted in the continental European tradition as the "rule of the majority," exercised in accordance with the "will of the majority," democracy can be and often has been quite tyrannical. Appreciation of this fact has provided a major impulse for constitution-making in our time. The inevitable conflict of such a democracy with constitutionalism has led some of the more ardently radical advocates of democracy to be anti-constitutionalists. But in countries that have been liberated by a sudden revolutionary act or comparable popular decision, the relations between the government and its subjects, between both of them and intermediary groups, can only be stably organized by a constitution.

That means fundamental rights must be enforceably protected and governmental powers divided and restrained. This contradiction in terms greatly complicates the paradox we stated at the outset. For in all communities which are not, like Britain, lucky in possessing a traditional frame of government that serves in its basic aspects as a constitution, whatever compromise is reached between the requirements of constitutionalism and the demands of democratism will remain tenuous and a constant source of tension and controversy.

This difficulty has been strongly appreciated by Israel's leadership. After some extended discussions, it was decided to follow the British example and allow the constitution "to grow." The present constitution of the state of Israel is therefore not embodied in a formal document, labeled *the constitution*, but consists of various statutes, customs, and practices which have developed during the years of the state's existence.[23] The democratic thrust was so strong in Israel that a legitimizing of the government by way of a constitution turned out to be quite unnecessary, in contrast to many other new nations' government.

[21] The notion of contrasting the "living constitution" with the formal document and its provisions has been widespread in the United States ever since Howard Lee McBain spoke of *The Living Constitution: A Constitution of the Realities and the Legends of our Fundamental Law*, 1929. Beyond and behind it stands the doctrine of the living law.

[22] The notion of the constitution as a facade is found in Löwenstein's *Political Power*, 1957. Cf. also my comments in my *Constitutional Government*, p. 602, with reference to Giovanni Sartori's (1962a) debate with W. H. Morris-Jones (1965) in *American Political Science Review*.

[23] Nadav Safran, *The United States and Israel*, 1963.

What it adds up to is that a constitution, any constitution, is not a panacea but an experimental attempt of arriving at a viable and legitimate government.[24] Even in the older countries, too few people realize that every constitution is continually changing, even without formal amendment, as is the case with law in general. For example, one might well ask whether the Fathers at Philadelphia, or the long line of judges who sat on the Supreme Court and other high courts, or even the congressmen and President were the "author" of the American Constitution. It may even be said that the Constitution as it exists today is the creation of the entire American people.

If constitution-making then is seen as a continuous process, it evidently is a meaningful and significant part of modern democratic government. In this light the mocking attitude of some political scientists toward "institutional" concern, in contrast to their own "behavioral" approach is rather misleading, since behavior and institutions are not mutually exclusive or antithetical terms referring to radically divergent realities. Quite to the contrary, institutions consist in established, repetitive behavior; the British Parliament is a group of human beings, elected by their countrymen, to do certain things, like electing a Prime Minister, and passing laws. Like the family and contract, to mention two familiar and widespread "institutions" of the law, parliament is a term with a general connotation of human beings doing these and related things, and behaving in certain more or less fixed ways.

A constitution presumably embodies a system of power relationships which has been effectively institutionalized. A constitution is basically a particular kind of law, and like all law it consists of enforced rules. It is a living system, dynamic and ever-changing, as was pointed out. Just as in an organic system, in a constitutional system the basic institutional pattern remains even though the component parts may undergo significant alterations.[25] Comparative constitutionalism seeks to determine the theoretical presuppositions and institutional manifestations of constitutional systems.[26]

---

[24] On legitimacy, cf. my *Man and His Government*, 1963b, Chapter 13, and Karl Löwenstein, *Political Reconstruction*, 1946, pp. 176 ff., where the author is primarily concerned with monarchical legitimacy.

[25] The third, fourth and fifth Republics of France, as well as the Weimar and Bonn Republic in Germany illustrate such persistence and continuity of a dynamic constitutional system; hence precedents remain valid from one to the other. Hitler's regime provides a striking contrast.

[26] See my *Constitutional Government*, and the review of writings on pp. 601 ff. To these I should like to add now C. F. Strong, *A History of Modern Political Constitutions*, 1963; unfortunately the work is very British in its outlook, and other writings are hardly mentioned. Among the French works of recent years, the new edition of Georges Burdeau's magistral *Traite de la Science Politique*, 2nd ed., 1967. The constitutional problems are dealt with in Vol. 4, 1967, and Vol. 2, 1967, pp. 29 ff. Cf. also Segundo V. Linares Quintana, *Derecho Constitucional e Instituciones Politicas*, 1960, Part 2, Chapters 3 and 4; Part 5; Part 6.

POWER
ITS
DISTRUST
AND
DISPERSION
2

THE CONCEPT OF POWER Constitutionalism by dividing power provides a system of effective restraints upon governmental action. In studying it, one has to explore the methods and techniques by which such restraints are established and maintained. Putting it another, more familiar, but less exact way, it is a body of rules ensuring fair play, thus rendering the government "responsible." There exist a considerable number of such techniques or methods.

The question confronts us: how did the idea of restraints arise? And who provided the support that made the idea victorious in many countries? [1] There are two important roots to the idea of restraints. One is the medieval heritage of natural-law doctrine. For while the royal bureaucrats gained the upper hand in fact, the other classes in the community who had upheld the medieval constitutionalism—the barons and the free towns, and above all the church—developed secularized versions of natural law. At the same time, they clung to residual institutions, such as the *parlements* in France. After the task of unification had been accomplished, and the despotic methods of absolutism could no longer be justified, these elements came forward with the idea of a separation of power. Both the English and the French revolutions served to dramatize these events.

The other root of the idea of restraints is shared by medieval and modern constitutionalism and is peculiar to some extent to Western culture. [2]

[1] The desire to fashion restraints for the rulers is, of course, quite ancient, and associated with the often religious sanctions for tradition; cf. Harry M. Orlinsky, *Ancient Israel*, 1954, Chapter 7. Many works of anthropologists, starting with the renowned Frazier, tell of such restraints.

[2] Catholic political philosophy, of course, has always stressed the idea of governmental restraints in connection with the Church's efforts to prevent secular ab-

It is Christianity, and more specifically the Christian doctrine of personality. The insistence upon the individual as the final value, the emphasis upon the transcendental importance of each man's soul, creates an insoluble conflict with any sort of absolutism. Here lies the core of the objection to all political conceptions derived from Aristotelian and other Greek sources. Since there exists a vital need for government just the same, this faith in the worth of each human being is bound to seek a balance of the two needs in some system of restraints which protects the individual, or at least minorities, against any despotic exercise of political authority. It is quite in keeping with this conflict that the apologists of unrestrained power have, in all ages of Western civilization, felt the necessity of *justifying* the exercise of such power, a necessity which was not felt elsewhere.

Nor was it felt by all in the West. Bacon and Hobbes, Bodin and Spinoza, and even Machiavelli insisted that some sort of inanimate force, such as reason, natural law, or enlightened self-interest would bring about a self-restraint. But a deep-seated distrust of power was part of the tradition that taught that "my Kingdom is not of this world," and that states are usually just "great robber bands," since they lack justice. Hence self-restraint of the ruler must be reinforced by effective institutions: restraints upon the arbitrary exercise of governmental power.

Modern constitutionalism then has always been linked with the problem of power, in theory as well as in practice. Historically, it constitutes a reaction against the concentration of power that accompanied the consolidation of modern states, dynastic and national. Its theorists have insisted on the importance of limiting and defining the power acquired by monarchs. While Hobbes described the rational structure of such a concentration of power and developed it into a veritable philosophy of power, Locke, taking up the challenge, demanded that the exercise of this power, although it was derived from the ultimate and unified source of all power—the people— remain divided by virtue of a fundamental decision.

Hobbes and Locke imply strongly divergent conceptions of power. Neither of these philosophers really clarified the nature of power in a very detailed way, although they both gave a roughly equivalent definition of it. Hobbes' overly broad definition as proposed in *Leviathan* identifies a man's power as "his present means to obtain some future apparent Good" (*Leviathan*, Chapter X). This is simply the human aspect of Hobbes' doctrine identifying power and force.[3] Such an identification of power with force does not

---

solutism. From St. Thomas to contemporary writers such as Jacques Maritain the idea has found ever new expression. See Heinrich A. Rommen's magistral *The State in Catholic Thought*, 1945. The stress, however, is upon natural law, and the role of institutional sanctions is minimized.

[3] Michael Oakshott in his Introduction to the edition of *Leviathan* (Oxford: Basil Blackwell, no date), p. xxi, has stressed this point.

take into account the most important aspect of power in the political and human sense, i.e., the fact that it is a relationship among human beings who may actually be freely cooperating. Hobbes' concept of power, which is still readily used by writers of politics who pride themselves on their "realism," treats power as if it were some kind of material substance, a thing like a bag of gold, on which you can sit and which you can possess.[4] The distinctive nature of political power cannot be understood in this perspective. The reason is that power presupposes common objectives, purposes, ends—objectives which are shared by two or more human beings. These objectives are called the values they cherish, the interests they pursue.

It is, therefore, impossible to study politics as the process of acquiring, distributing, and losing power without taking into consideration the major objectives, purposes, or ends of the human beings involved in power situations. Philosophers since Plato and Aristotle have claimed that these ends are relatively stable, that goodness or happiness, and also duty, constitute the ultimate value on which such a hierarchy of ends is erected. One readily believes that one can speak of ends in general terms. Such discourse may be metaphysical, arrived at through philosophical dialectic, or it may be derived from the "common agreement of all men."

If it may be taken as axiomatic that political power is related to objectives and presupposes several human beings (indeed, typically, a group of human beings who are sharing such objectives), it would appear that power is characteristically power *in a community*.[5] From this vantage point, it can be seen that power *is* a certain kind of human relationship, and not, as I have said, merely a material thing.

But what is the nature of this relationship? Can one demonstrate the existence of a fundamental characteristic common to all power? A well-known political scientist in cooperation with a philosopher defined power in this way in a recent work: "Participation in the making of decisions."[6] He accepts the idea that power is a relationship and not a possession. But one can still ask whether the participation in a decision is the crucial aspect of the power relationship. Undoubtedly it is implied in it, and anyone can agree that the proposition "G has power over H, compared to value K" would imply that G participates in the elaboration of decisions affecting the conduct of H with regard to K. But this does not necessarily exhaust the problem of the existential structure of power. In order to clarify the question of power, it is

---

[4] Hobbes was forced to this view of reason. It is a calculation, an addition, a subtraction, etc. (*Leviathan*, Chapter 5).

[5] Hereafter, when the word *power* is used, it is always taken to mean political power. We are not here concerned with physical power (force) at all.

[6] Harold D. Lasswell and Abraham Kaplan, *Power and Society*, 1950, p. 75.

useful to come back to the concept of power considered as a material possession.[7]

There can be no question that in numerous situations (and probably always), power does, to a certain degree, have this quality of a material substance. This is especially true wherever the holding of established and institutionalized offices brings with it the possession of power in the sense of the capacity to force compliance through decisions taken by him who possesses the particular office. This power to force compliance is hence universally recognized as the "power of office," and already shows why a definition of power in terms of a participating in decisions will not suffice. From this set of facts has sprung the tendency of many practical jurists and politologists to think of power essentially as the power to command, that is, to order around, with all the unfortunate misconceptions which the term "power politics" implies.

We should add a brief word about the relationship of conceptions of power to ethical and moral considerations. Everyone knows Lord Acton's saying: "All power tends to corrupt, and absolute power corrupts absolutely." It is often forgotten that Acton used the more prudent expression: "*tends* to corrupt." But he added the severe phrase: "Great men are almost always bad men, even when they exercise influence and not authority: still more, when you superadd the tendency or the certainty of corruption by authority." And in order to make sure that the serious nature of his accusation is not ignored, he adds: "There is no worse heresy than that the office sanctifies the holder of it." [8] Acton includes both office and authority in his moral qualms about power. He expresses a feeling which has been the basis of Western constitutionalism at least since Locke's time. Locke's Calvinist forerunners had similar feelings. As a matter of fact, the idea that a good government must be limited by law can be traced back to the Middle Ages. Moreover, the medieval perspective helps one to remember Acton's thoughts on power and on the evil to be found in its manifestations which has a profoundly religious connotation. Christian anxiety about this world, the concept of original sin, reveals the ontological implications of this attitude.

To note the cosmic implications of Lord Acton's affirmation has value for our work only if it helps to clarify that power not only tends to corrupt but is also the only ground on which finite men can proceed in order to be good. More simply stated, *man can do only as much good as his power allows.* The office certainly does not sanctify its holder, but great Church Fathers, such as Saint Augustine and Saint Ambroise, certainly held office. Need we

---

[7] This notion of Hobbes is Bertrand Russell's perspective in his book *Power*, 1938; it is also that of Talcott Parsons in his book *The Social System*, 1950.

[8] Cf. the Acton-Creighton correspondence, republished in *Essays on Freedom and Power*, 1948, p. 364.

add that they were certainly not "bad men," in any comparative sense? It is clear that Lord Acton had in mind the type of thought attributed to Jesus in the New Testament when he suggests that it is easier for a poor man to go to heaven than it is for a rich man, for if wealth corrupts, power, a form of wealth, also corrupts by multiplying opportunities for selfish actions.

Let us now come back to the nature of power relations. If we grant that power may be a material substance, something one can have and touch, it is equally true that power (*dynamis*) is continuously generated, that it is in a state of becoming. Cooperation among members of a group underscores this second aspect. Power is not inherent in some of the members of the group, but rather is inherent in the relations themselves which bind the group together and make it a community.

We must also understand how such power is generated. That element of power which appears analogous to a material possession is clearly rooted in force. It is an extension of natural power, physical and mental force used to make other men submit to him who possesses power. Man's force increases in proportion to his power. Subjection of this kind implies violence or constraint. It is clear that power is continuously generated by successful constraint, that this constraint implies physical, economic, or spiritual weapons; military and economic force; or force of an intellectual and emotional nature.

Conformance and compliance then can be forced in many ways. However, such analysis leaves one unsatisfied, since it is clear that these behaviors can also come about through spontaneous and voluntary cooperation, through the meeting of bodies and minds, in short, through consent rather than constraint. Although one may grant that a considerable twilight zone exists, situations of evident consent and situations of evident constraint are clearly distinguishable. There is no doubt that voluntary compliance also generates power.

Locke emphasizes this consensual aspect of power; he points out that any use of force must be applied with a view toward the common good. For him, as for a great tradition going back through the scholastics to the Ancients, the term "common good" implies that consent has really sanctioned the actions of those who possess power. That is, those in question would comply voluntarily or sanction the use of force if they could be put in a position to judge the affair at its true value.[9] Indeed any lawful governmental power is based on consent; this may be the direct explicit consent of the majority of those who have chosen to become or to remain members of a community and who are consequently willing to accept the decisions, that is, the actions of the majority; or such consent may be indirect and implicit.

---

[9] Cf. J. W. Gough's commentary in his interesting study *John Locke's Political Philosophy*, 1950, pp. 30 ff., in which he presents a critique of Willmore Kendall's work on consent, *John Locke and the Doctrine of Majority Rule*, 1941.

Without considering the normative aspect of the matter implied in a lawful government, it is clear that not all power is a result of consent, but it is also clear that certain forms of power are. Without pursuing further the problem of the precise nature of such consent (intrinsically implying something spontaneous, voluntary, etc.), it would seem useful to add that consent is not simply non-constraint (just as constraint is not merely non-consent.)

Consent and constraint are real forces psychologically. They both generate power. When we say that they generate power, we refer to all of those relationships between human beings whereby their actions become coordinated and constitute a single force. In real-life situations, all the more complex power situations (such as a government involves), invariably rest upon both consent and constraint. To put it in a more abstract form, power by mere consent and power by mere constraint are "unreal" limits between which the power situations of actual life oscillate.[10]

THE DIVISION OF POWER

The doctrine of the division of power was developed by Locke and Montesquieu. This doctrine has been widely criticized in Europe and the United States. It has been said that Montesquieu was wrong when he asserted that the division of power was a fundamental characteristic of the British constitution which he admired, since it was a limited monarchy. In fact, Montesquieu was almost correct. He based his argument on what was generally believed to be the constitutional situation in England after the Glorious Revolution. Montesquieu used Locke's doctrine but very ingeniously transformed it.

Locke's scheme revolves around the legislative power that he believed to be of central importance and hence something to be divided between king, Lords, and Commons who, however, act together in and through Parliament. In other words, Locke's separation of powers doctrine focuses attention upon the division of *one* power, rather than a division of the powers, as distinguished from each other. Locke also distinguished an executive and a federative power, but he placed these in the hands of the king. The executive and federative power, he says, ought not to be "separated and placed in the hands of distinctive persons." He thus remained very close to the traditional British constitution. The reason for this, says Locke, is that "they require the force of the society for their exercise," and so "to try to separate them would some time or other cause disorder and ruin."

It is of utmost importance that at the base of the separation of power Locke saw the power of the community at large, and since the latter is

[10] Three basic hypotheses are developed in my *Constitutional Government and Politics*, 1932, pp. 15–18. They are concerned with the intensity of a political situation, the degree of power concentration, and "anticipated reactions."

generated by the general consent which expresses itself in the social contract, the derivative powers are clothed with substantial compulsion. The constraint on which they depend makes them possessions, gives them the character of something to be had or held, and consequently makes them something that can be divided in accord with the will of the community which may be said "always to be the supreme power."

Montesquieu's transformation of Locke's scheme arises in part from the fact that his interest in the problem of consent, or rather of power, is considerably less intense. As already stated, it is also the result of the wish to give a distinct and independent role to the judiciary. Montesquieu transforms the executive into the judicial power (the latter having been included in the executive by Locke), and develops the federative power into the executive, by broadening its security and defense tasks into a more general proposition. The crucial passage in Montesquieu reads as follows: "There is no freedom at all if the power to judge is not separate from legislative and executive power. If it were joined to executive power, the judge would have the force of an oppressor." [11]

In his transformation of the power scheme, Montesquieu no longer emphasizes legislative power, as Locke had done, but rather stresses the division of the three powers. Of course, his famous statement that "all would be lost if the same man or body of principals or nobles, or men from among the people, exercised these three powers . . ." [12] could still be squared with Locke's scheme. But actually Montesquieu begins with a positive statement and insists that each power mentioned be in the hands of a different body or person. It is clear that this can only be accomplished by a constituent power which establishes such an order.

The idea of constitutionalism in the specific modern sense had finally emerged. It rests upon the distrust of power. It is evident that another power, one and indivisible, must stand behind the powers that are to be divided. This is the power to make the Constitution, to establish the constitutional order, and in case of need, to amend it, modify it, and even replace it with another one.

In these last statements the word power is used in two divergent connotations, according to what has been said above about power. For when one refers to constituent power, power basically means relational power generated by consent. Whereas when those powers are considered that have been divided by the constitution, power is largely understood as a thing to possess and to be regarded as susceptible to division and transfer.

[11] Cf. the famous Chapter 6 of Book 11 of Montesquieu's *De l'Esprit des Lois*, 1748.

[12] Montesquieu, *De l'Esprit des Lois:* "Tout seroit perdu si le même homme, ou le même corps des principaux ou des nobles, ou du peuple, exerçoient ces trois pouvoirs . . ."

The distribution of derivative powers flows from the initial generating act of the constituent power. In the decisive constitutionalist period from the end of the seventeenth century to the nineteenth century, this basic power was believed to be the inalienable possession of the people. At least it was so believed by all those who rejected the conservative notions of divine grace which vindicated this basic power for the monarch. Such ideas now seem so outdated that it might be useful to recall that many constitutions, even in the nineteenth century, began their preamble by asserting precisely this divinely ordained authority of the monarch to give his people a constitution. But those who claimed that in fact the people themselves had this power, had the better of the argument. The "people" might in reality be only a limited group from *among* the people. A realistic appraisal of what actually happens when a constitution is made obliges us to recognize that there exists an unorganized residual power of resistance in any community. This residual power attempts to restrain and often does restrain the government. It comes into play when the government fails to function. In short, any community contains a certain number of persons who make up a considerable part of the basic and most intelligent portion of the community who usually participate in the making of vital decisions. To the extent that the survival of the community depends on their cooperation, they are likely to be able to make good their demands for such a participation. It can be seen here that the problem of power is related to that of powerlessness; for if the community itself disintegrates, whatever power it generated will also disappear. This is the kernel of truth that democratic theory stresses when it speaks of the inalienable rights of the people.[13]

Because the people, or rather that part of the people which succeeds in speaking for it, possesses this residual power resulting from common consent, it is only natural that political parties in developed constitutionalist systems must to a certain degree reintegrate the powers that have been separated by the constitution. This fact is not, as has often been claimed, proof of the unsoundness of the constitutional ordering of powers and their separation, but quite the contrary: it shows that the idea of a constitutional division of powers is rooted in the concept of an integrated ordering power which serves to organize the community for political action. This constituent power is the equivalent of the notion of the sovereign in earlier political theory, but it should not be identified with it. For the classic definition of a sovereign (Bodin, Hobbes, Austin) always emphasizes his omni-competence, that is to say, the fact that he has the last word on any matter he wishes to deal with. The constituent power, on the other hand, only orders the exercise of power in the constitutionalized community and nothing more, just as the

---

[13] Cf. the interesting discussion in Charles Merriam's book, *Power*, 1936, Chapter 6, entitled "The Poverty of Power."

amending power only modifies the existing constitution according to the procedure set down by the constitution. The parties, by effectuating a substantial measures of coordination among the power wielders within the framework of a constitution, are reminiscent of, so to speak, the residual power of the "people" on which the whole order rests.

We are purposely omitting any detailed discussion of the actual patterns of the separation of power such as can be found in different states. But a brief word about federalism is in order. Federalism constitutes a particular kind of division of power. Like the functional division of power, it too is characteristically an *ordering* of the exercise of power within a community. It is, however, a particular kind of community, namely a composite one in which distinct territorial subcommunities exist. They may have resulted from the differentiation of a previous single community, as in the British Commonwealth or post-Nazi Germany, or they may be the actual constituent component communities of an emerging larger community. In either case, the need for combining unity with diversity, of recognizing the existence of a community composed of communities, leads to an ordering of the exercise of power which, in fact, divides power between the inclusive community and its component and constituent communities. They each retain, under a constitution, a certain amount of the constituent power and therefore characteristically order autonomously their own internal exercise of power over those matters which the constitution leaves to them.[14] From the vantage point of this analysis of power under constitutionalism, federalism appears to be a spatial or territorial separation and division of power. It, too, undergoes a certain amount of effective integration or at least coordination as a result of the influence of party politics. Since the parties are both national and local, and under federalism possess a structure which recognizes the autonomy of the local leadership, such integration is necessarily limited.

Taking into account these several patterns of the separation and division of power, and bearing in mind that any recognition of an autonomous sphere of the citizen as guaranteed under modern constitutions also constitutes a "separation of powers,"[15] we are now able to state the nature of a constitution in terms of power. A constitution, then, is the *ordering and dividing* of the exercise of political power by that group in an existent community who are able to secure the consent of the community and who thereby make manifest the power of the community itself. It is decisive that the power be divided and not concentrated in the hands of those acting

[14] For federalism as a highly dynamic process resulting from these interacting powers of a composite community, see below, Chapter 5.

[15] The power aspect of the bills of rights has often been overlooked, but has recently been brought into focus by the abuse made of these "powers" by subversive groups of citizens.

on behalf of the community; if the latter is done, if the exercise of power is concentrated in the hands of the organizing group—as has repeatedly been the case after revolutions—the group so acting is not a constituent, that is to say, a constitution-making group, but an autocratic, anticonstitutional conqueror.[16] This is evidently the case of the totalitarian movements of our time which, even when they give lip-service to the constitutional tradition, show no inclination to divide power, but on the contrary, concentrate it in their own hands.

Constitutions evidently have a function which is realized in the process of constitution-making, constitution-amending, and constitution-interpreting: it is the function of rendering a government responsible by establishing and maintaining effective regularized restraints upon political, and more especially upon governmental, action. The stress laid upon "effective" restraints seeks to focus attention upon the fact that a seeming constitutional order may in fact be nothing of the kind. The existence of formally legal restraints is in no way an indication of the existence of a constitutional order in the political sense.[17] Likewise, the absence of formal laws, embodying such restraints, does not mean that they are lacking. The effective restraints of the British constitution are found in such practices as the alternation of parties and related constitutional conventions and not in a formal separation of powers. They are nonetheless in keeping with our characterization of a constitution.

To conclude, it has been shown how modern constitutionalism is a very particular way of distributing power, by organizing its division, its "checking and balancing," as the conventional formula has it. The customary view has been shown to be based upon too one-sided a view of "power" as merely a possession. Against this view, a conception of power has been outlined which recognizes its dual nature and duly stresses its mutual, relational aspect which is shown to be more basic than the proprietary, "corporeal," or material side. Behind and beneath all the different kinds of schemes for dividing and separating the exercise of power there is found the common power of the community, the "pool" as it were, from which the fountains are fed that make manifest the existence of the pool. Power probably *is*, ontologically speaking, an attribute of all being; it certainly is an attribute of all political being. It can be understood only as the projection of a

---

[16] By the expression "barbarians from within," Arnold Toynbee has dramatically signalized this aspect of conquest in such groups.

[17] This issue is at the core of a very interesting controversy between W. H. Morris-Jones and Giovanni Sartori. Sartori had adversely commented on British views of constitutionalism, in "Constitutionalism: A Preliminary Discussion," 1962a. Morris-Jones undertook to defend part of this tradition in "On Constitutionalism," 1965, where the rejoinder of Sartori is found, pp. 441 ff. Cf. my comments in *Constitutional Government and Democracy*, 1968a, pp. 601 ff.

community's very existence. If constitutionalism were really an attempt to deny this unitary source of power, it would be the empty formal structure which its enemies have alleged it to be. Actually, it is a particular form of this power of a community, a form which results from the fact that those composing the community and more especially the community's leaders prize highly one value above all others. That value is freedom.[18] Because they value freedom they distrust all power.

[18] For the complexities of this term, and the three dimensions of freedom, see my *Man and His Government*, 1963b, Chapters 20 and 21.

CONSTITUTIONAL-ISM AND LIBERTY

3

"Man is born free!" This is the trumpet call of modern political thought, and more especially of the American and French revolutions. Liberty, the members of the American Congress proclaimed on July 4, 1776, is one of the basic and inalienable rights, besides life and the pursuit of happiness.[1] It is a common misunderstanding to think that great historical events, such as the Declaration of Independence and the constitution-making that followed it, spring from social life and man's initiative without precedent. In fact, events of this sort have a long seed-time during which ideas crystallize and eventually influence human actions. This observation applies with particular force to constitutional liberty. The seeds that germinated before the American Revolution and blossomed in the great document that is the American Constitution were planted over a long period of time. Some of them go back to classical antiquity.

That a good government should be a government of laws and not of men is an overstatement of the classical notion that a government should be operating according to law. Plato and Aristotle both maintained that it did so operate whenever it was ethically sound. These thinkers were not, however, bothered by the modern idea of individual rights. It was a matter of a well-ordered community in which justice prevailed, and the good life was thriving that preoccupied them. This fact is basic to the contrast between ancient and modern constitutionalism.[2] Pericles in his immortal

[1] Cf. Carl Becker, *The Declaration of Independence,* 1942; Bernard Bailyn, *The Ideological Origins of the American Revolution,* 1967. Cf. also (for the documents) Carl J. Friedrich and Robert G. McCloskey, *From the Declaration of Independence to the Constitution,* 1954.

[2] Charles H. McIlwain, *Constitutionalism: Ancient and Modern,* 1940. McIlwain does not sufficiently stress the difference. See for greater detail on this issue Carl J. Friedrich, *Transcendent Justice,* 1964, Chapter 1.

funeral oration celebrates the freedom of the men who died in the defense of freedom. But we do not hear of human rights, but of freedom as independence and happiness in being "lovers of beauty and of wisdom." [3] The citizen of a Greek city or of Rome had no freedom of conviction and belief. Far from it; he was expected to accept and live by the religion of his city, to honor its gods and observe its rituals.[4] Only the coming of Christianity raised this crucial issue, for as Christian thought moved away from the dogmatism of earlier thinkers like St. Augustine, a greater emphasis on toleration occurred. With it came as well the notion that rulers and ruled were bound to each other on the basis of reciprocal loyalties.

Britain was at the head of the development of modern constitutionalism. Why this was so is not entirely clear. Probably many different factors combined to make possible the steady deepening and expansion of a particular political culture among the English-speaking people. The English revolution came early into modern constitutionalism. Ever since, British constitutionalism has been more traditionalist than rationalist in its foundations. Eventually, in the sixteenth and seventeenth centuries, the merchant class became predominant; at first it supported the Tudor kings against the feudal aristocracy, but eventually it no longer needed the monarchy.

The revolutionary struggle finally produced the new constitutional order that has been developing uninterruptedly in England ever since. During two full generations the whole range of political issues, from absolutism in Hobbes to anarchy in the Levellers, was explored, fought over with word and sword, and finally settled in favor of a division of power between king, Lords, and Commons. This order, although it sounded medieval and traditionalist, was in fact modern in that the real foundation of this division was the electorate behind the Commons, rather than the ecclesiastical authorities and feudal landowners behind the Lords. It was the Commons who from then on were to restrain the exercise of the Crown's power, reinforced by independent courts. After the Commons had, in the eighteenth century, become the real core of the government, the division was maintained through the recognition of the opposition, the basis of the party system.

The idea of liberty and that of constitutionalism are closely related in English tradition. Liberty, in the political sense of the word, always means liberty within or under a constitution. But no provision at all is made for concepts such as those derived from Rousseau and developed by the Jacobins

[3] Thucydides, *Peloponnesian War*, Book 2, Chapters 35 ff. and more especially Chapter 43.

[4] Jakob Burckhardt, *Griechische Kulturgeschichte*, 4 vols., ed. Deri, 1898 and later; Fustel de Coulanges, *The Ancient City*, 7th ed. tr. by Willard Small, 1889 (Boston: Lee & Shepard), especially Chapter 17. See Eric A. Havelock, *The Liberal Temper in Greek Politics*, 1957, especially the concluding chapter.

which demand unlimited power for certain communities, such as the nation. Thus the constitutional concept became the most characteristic element of the political thought of the English-speaking world.

Logic now demands that one define what is meant by a constitution. A constitution or division of power provides a system of effective restraints upon governmental action. In studying it, one has to explore the methods and techniques by which such restraints are established and maintained. Putting it in another, more familiar, but less exact way, a constitution is a body of rules ensuring fair play, thus rendering the government "responsible." There exist a considerable number of such techniques or methods, and they will receive fuller treatment in the appropriate place.

The English began very early to realize that there was a difference between their own institutions and those prevailing on the continent. Discussions on this subject usually took the form of a contrast with France, the country the English knew best and liked the least. In fact, toward the end of the Middle Ages, at the end of the long struggle of the Hundred Years' War, brightened for the French by the heroic figure of Joan of Arc, a strong feeling of antagonism toward their neighbors on the continent had anchored itself in the English mind.

A "government with estates" was widespread in medieval Europe.[5] One found it not only in England and France, but also in Spain and Sweden, in Poland and Hungary, in the various German principalities, and even in the Empire itself. Therefore, it is a mistake to think that the parliament is an original and specifically British institution, as liberal historians, especially British and American, have had us believe: many different countries in the Middle Ages had estates' assemblies which took an active part in legislation and other governmental action.

What, in a general sense, was the nature of this "medieval constitutionalism"? Like any constitutionalism worthy of the name, it puts the government *under* the law. At the same time, it makes the ecclesiastical authorities the guardians of the "law." [6] Legislation played only a secondary role in the medieval governmental process. Laws were few and legislation rare, and medieval constitutionalism could thus concentrate its attention on the problem of the regulation of the abuse of the monarchic executive's power.

Another important element in the growth of constitutionalism is the rather widespread tendency to recognize the people's right to resist a lawless government. The right of resistance was omnipresent in the medieval

---

[5] On the government with estates (*Staendestaat*) consult my *Constitutional Government and Democracy*, 1968a, Chapter 14; and Otto Brunner, *Law und Herrschaft: Grundfragen der territoriaten Verfassungsgeschichte Oesterreichs im Mittelalter*, 4th ed., 1959 (Vienna).

[6] Charles H. McIlwain, *The High Court of Parliament and Its Supremacy*, 1910. See also J. G. A. Pocock, *The Ancient Constitution and the Feudal Law*, 1947.

social order, on the continent as well as in England.[7] However, it was in England that the right was given its most extensive and articulate justification. It is characteristic that the struggle over Tudor absolutism occurred over the requirement of an oath by which the English public servant would recognize that no earthly power was superior to that of the king. This meant, in fact, that the king had a right to his subjects' loyalty, even though his acts might be criticized by the Pope and ecclesiastical authority as unlawful. This was the issue in the struggle between Henry VIII and Sir Thomas More. The fact that the king's matrimonial vagaries were a key issue in this struggle gave a certain spice to this formal argument.

Elizabeth I, though more moderate, was also prepared to demand an oath of supremacy to herself. But she was scrupulously concerned about the formal rights of her subjects and, in particular, of her Parliament. Sir Thomas Smith and Richard Hooker, thoughtful theorists, discussed her intelligently balanced system of government; it became known from the ecclesiastical point of view as the "Elizabethan Settlement." Smith and Hooker played a key role in the evolution of the idea of constitutional liberty. Let us look first at Sir Thomas Smith (1513–1577).

Smith was a learned man, a humanist, jurist, and magistrate. A small book entitled *De Republica Anglorum* contains the quintessence of his thought. Written before 1568, at least in part, but published only after the author's death in 1583, this work became the classic source on England's parliamentary institutions, not only in England but also abroad. Smith does not yet distinguish between Parliament and the king. He speaks of the tradition of the supreme power as the "King in Parliament." He was a member of Parliament when the Act of Supremacy was proclaimed, with the significant title: "An Act restoring to the Crown the ancient jurisdiction over the State ecclesiastical and spiritual, and abolishing all foreign power repugnant to the same."[8] However, once this absolute supremacy of the Crown was established, always conjointly, of course, with the Parliament—in keeping

---

[7] Kurt Wolzendorf, *Staatsrecht and Naturrecht in der Lehre vom Widerstandsrecht des Volkes,* 1916.

[8] The main passages on this subject are found in Chapter 7 of *De Republica Anglorum:* ". . . no foreign prince, person, prelate, state or potentate, spiritual or temporal, shall at any time after the last day of this session of Parliament, use, enjoy or exercise any manner of power, jurisdiction, superiority, authority, pre-eminence or privilege, spiritual or ecclesiastical, within this realm or any other of your Majesty's dominions. . . ." And in Chapter 8 one reads the following: ". . . such jurisdictions, privileges, superiorities, and pre-eminences, spiritual and ecclesiastical, as by any spiritual or ecclesiastical power or authority hath heretofore been or may lawfully be exercised or used for the visitation of the ecclesiastical state and persons, and for reformation, order and correction of the same and of all manner of errors, heresies, schisms, abuses, offences, contempts and enormities, shall for ever, by authority of this present Parliament, be united and annexed to the Imperial crown of this realm. . . ."

with English tradition—the problem of constitutionalism arose once again. Sir Thomas Smith was the first to try to resolve it. He defines a "Commonwealth" [9] as a "society or common doing of a multitude of free men collected together and united by common accord and covenants among themselves, for the conservation of themselves as well in peace as in war." [10]

Thus, in his framework of traditional thought, Sir Thomas Smith declares that "the most high and absolute power of the realm of England consisteth in the Parliament." But it must be noted that when Sir Thomas Smith speaks of the Parliament he is speaking of the "King in Parliament" and at the end of this essential chapter he adds that "every Englishman is intended to be there present, either in person or by procuration and attorney, of what preeminence, state, dignity or quality soever he be, from the Prince (be he King or Queen) to the lowest person of England." [11] Smith adds the following significant words: "And the consent of the Parliament is taken to be every man's consent." What this means is that the nation is a *corpus mysticum* expressing itself through the intermediary of the king in Parliament.

Smith goes on to speak in detail about the parliamentary process, the core of the nation's life and existence. And he finally comes to the crucial issue of every constitutional system: the distribution and separation of power.[12] He presents a long discussion of judicial power which he shows to be partially parliamentary and partially royal. There is a very clear acceptance of a division or separation of power between the king and Parliament. The essential power, the legislative one, is considered to be exercised conjointly by the king and Parliament. In supporting this idea of a traditional division of authority between the king and the Parliament, Smith reaffirms earlier arguments of writers like Fortescue in favor of a *constitutional* royal regime (*dominium regale politicum*). This view was clearly opposed to the tendency on the continent in favor of absolutism and in support of a theory of sovereignty clearly freeing royal rule from all restraints.

But Sir Thomas Smith leaves open the very question which became the center of later revolutionary controversies, namely, what happens in case of disagreement between the king and Parliament. The revolutionaries were to claim that Parliament held supreme power, that is, had the last word. Such an opinion would have sounded very strange indeed to a high official in Elizabethan England.

[9] The term "Commonwealth" is here understood in the republican sense which was its meaning at that time in England.

[10] Sir Thomas Smith, *De Republica Anglorum*, Chapter 10.

[11] Smith, *De Republica Anglorum*, Book 2, Chapter 1 (in G. W. Prothero, ed., *Select Statutes and Other Constitutional Documents Illustrative of the Reigns of Elizabeth and James I*, 4th ed., 1913, p. 128).

[12] He sums up his ideas in Book 2, Chapter 4.

When Sir Edward Coke (1552–1634) undertook to treat these problems, the issue had become much more precise. The previous constitutional concept of a harmony of power had to be abandoned and replaced by the modern concept of a delegation of power originating from a sovereign source of power.[13] In his quality of jurist and magistrate, he had come into conflict with the king in the past on the basis of the traditional constitutional concept. But the pressure of circumstances forced him to abandon the idea of harmony and balance in the constitution to consider the problem of supremacy, and finally to declare the supremacy of Parliament. A fact that has escaped many authors is that this is the logical consequence of the elimination of ecclesiastic authority which had played more or less efficiently the role of balancing the constitution of medieval society. For harmony was not considered to be natural according to the teachings of the Church. Thus, when the ancient balance was destroyed, it was necessary to find a new base for supreme authority.

Coke displays judicial conservatism in his view of Magna Carta. In it he saw, with exceptional insistence, the foundation of the rights of the English in Parliament. The traditional interpretation which makes Magna Carta out to be a charter of human rights dates back to him. Historically Magna Carta was in fact nothing more than a charter of established feudal rights and privileges. But Coke boldly formulated a principle of constitutional interpretation that has become fundamental in the thought of the English-speaking world: ". . . for that which has been refined and perfected by the wisest men in former succession of ages, and proved and approved by continual experience, that cannot but with risk of great hazard and danger be altered or changed." [14] Above all, he claimed that the Tudors, secretly, and the Stuarts, more openly, had introduced and were continuing to introduce dangerous modifications. "Parliament" had the exclusive right to modify England's laws, and it was necessary vigorously to oppose any claim on the part of the king tending to undertake such changes by himself. Coke asked that the "Magna Charta and these Acts be put in due execution and that all alegements, awards, and rules given or to be given to the contrary shall be void. . . ." [15]

In his famous work *Institutes of the Laws of England*, Coke briefly describes his idea of the English government. He expresses his opinion regarding the supremacy of the Parliament (as the highest court) in a some-

---

[13] George H. Sabine, *A History of Political Theory*, rev. ed., 1954, pp. 451 ff.

[14] See my *The Philosophy of Law in Historical Perspective*, 2nd ed., 1963c, Chapter 10, especially at p. 79. Consult Coke's introductory essay to Book 4 of his *Institutes*, and his *Reports*, 12, pp. 64–65.

[15] The relevant documents are found in G. W. Prothero, *Select Statutes*, 1913, and Samuel R. Gardiner, *Constitutional Documents of the Puritan Revolution, 1625–1660*, 3rd ed., 1906.

what more energetic manner than Smith.[16] "The jurisdiction of this court is so transcendent that it maketh, enlargeth, diminisheth, abrogateth, repealeth, and reviveth laws, statutes, acts, and ordinances, concerning matters ecclesiastical, capital, criminal, common, civil, marital, and the rest."

Stress was laid upon procedure. At the occasion of the struggle for the Petition of Right when King Charles tried to resolve the issue informally, Parliament was opposed to this. "This is a session of Parliament," they declared, "and therefore must take His Majesty's word no otherwise than in a parliamentary way only and in no other way; that is to say, with regard to a question, that is of a matter agreed on by both Houses, His Majesty sitting on his throne in his robe with his crown on his head, sceptre in his hand, and in full Parliament. . . ."[17] Note that the king is required to follow the detailed procedural rules which regulate his participation in the legislative process!

It is appropriate to mention briefly another point that illustrates the change leading toward the discovery of a new basis for supremacy or for sovereignty, the doctrine according to which a future Parliament can never be bound by a preceding Parliament. In a certain sense this is the most spectacular aspect of the Parliament's legislative power. Coke expresses this idea clearly in his study on the Parliament: ". . . although several Parliaments have tried to paralyze, restrain, suspend, modify or annul the work of later Parliaments, they never could succeed; for the following Parliament always has the power to repeal, suspend, modify, make explicit or annul the work of a preceding one, in whole or in part. . . ." That is why Magna Charta itself can be modified by a Parliament but not by the king. In terms of constitutional theory, Parliament, as it incarnates the nation's *corpus mysticum,* can modify the constitution; Parliament is not under its control but, on the contrary, it is master of the constitution. It possesses what is now called the power of amendment which is part of its legislative sovereignty.

To sum up the contrast offered by the English and French trends of this period: the Parliaments of the Middle Ages, which were primarily courts, found themselves confronted with the fact that law had increasingly to be *made* rather than discovered and declared. In France the king claimed this right to make law as one of his prerogatives, with the *parlement* retaining only the right to record royal edicts. This was not the evolution in England. Throughout the entire Tudor reign as well as that of the Stuarts, Parliament was in a position to insist upon its right to participate in the legislative process. In fact, later the Commons preferred to abandon part of their judicial power, which was to a large extent in the hands of the Lords, rather

---

[16] See for this the documents in Gardiner, *Constitutional Documents,* esp. pp. 66 ff.

[17] Gardiner, *Constitutional Documents,* pp. 66 ff.

than to lose even a portion of its legislative prerogatives. The struggle over this "prerogative" was at the center of the problem of the respective roles of the king and the Parliament with regard to legislation.

The battle cry in these long, drawn-out struggles over law and the constitution in the course of which the idea of human rights crystallized was liberty. Two rights seemed to lie in the center of man's liberty: the right to his property and the right to his conscience. The time-hallowed phrase of Englishmen which speaks of a man's home as his castle stresses this point. Property is as important in the evolution of constitutional liberty as religious freedom. Their linkage in seventeenth-century England was paramount to the effective institutionalizing of human liberty.

Western man's interest in history has often taken the road of exploring the rise of ideas and ideologies. Constitutionalism has been traced in its relation to liberalism, to rationalism, to individualism. Each one of these general philosophies has indeed contributed its fair share to the making of constitutionalism. But a different perspective results from these several ideologies. Liberalism, the most recent of the three, is certainly at variance with socialism; hence if constitutionalism is linked with liberalism, it seems reasonable to conclude that it is about to pass away. Rationalism is the most general and is associated with many different forms of culture; if constitutionalism is the political outgrowth of rationalism, it acquires a more universal significance. But rationalism has been dominant in societies the political order of which did not much resemble modern constitutionalism. Again, individualism crystallized in the period when modern constitutionalism began to take shape. To this individualism, constitutionalism owes the distinguishing feature of modern, in contrast to ancient and medieval, constitutionalism.

Liberty is a core value not only for liberalism, but for rationalism and individualism as well. Because this is so, all three ideologies relate to constitutionalism, for freedom of the individual is compatible with the freedom of all under law. Its exercise presupposes effective institutions which provide the restraint without which power—the power of the individual, of the group, and of the state—tends to be abused. "The only purpose for which power can be rightfully exercised over any member of a civilized community against his will is to prevent harm to others," wrote John Stuart Mill in his *Liberty*. Only a good constitution can provide that. At this point, there arises the possibility of a clash between liberty and democracy, and to this problem we now turn.

CONSTITUTIONAL-ISM AND DEMOCRACY

4

The terms constitutional democracy and democratic constitutionalism have in recent years come increasingly into usage and are almost slogans by now. To many Americans these terms seem either contradictions or pleonasms. For, say some, what is democracy but a constitutional order such as exists in the United States, whereas others would insist that if a regime is a constitutional one, it cannot be a democracy. This would have been the opinion of most of the Founding Fathers, notably the more conservative ones. It rests upon the notion that a democracy is the kind of radical rule of the popular majority which Jean Jacques Rousseau had developed in his *Social Contract*.

Most Americans at the start of this century understood democracy to mean the kind of constitutional order that prevailed in the United States and Great Britain in which the popular majority was restrained in many ways. The rise of totalitarian regimes, such as the Soviet Union and Fascist Germany which claimed to be democracies, which indeed proclaimed themselves as perfect democracies,[1] made it necessary to differentiate between such totalitarian "democracies" and the Western variety which came to be called constitutional democracy. The totalitarians themselves preferred to call the Western regimes capitalist democracies or plutocracies.[2]

[1] Stalin, in a speech on February 6, 1946, sharply expressed this contrast. Adam Ulam, in his magisterial *Expansion and Coexistence—The History of Soviet Foreign Policy, 1917–1967*, 1968, does not stress this speech, but see his Chapter 9 for the same issue.

[2] The issue was raised in the 1937 edition of my *Constitutional Government and Politics*, but did not have much echo, perhaps because of the radically democratic atmosphere which the New Deal brought on. The issue was highlighted by J. L. Talmon, *The Rise of Totalitarian Democracy*, 1952, especially Chapter 3 of Part I, though his interpretation of Rousseau must be questioned.

No clarification of this semantic tangle could be hoped for without a firmer understanding of what is meant by a constitution, and the marked difference between the United States and Great Britain on this score complicated such clarification. For on the face of it Britain does not have a written constitution, nor a bill of rights, nor a separation of powers. Actually these appearances are deceptive; for the British constitution is of course "written" but not codified into one document; a bill of rights has existed since at least 1688 although it does not by any means contain all the rights of Britishers,[3] and a separation of powers has existed for a long time, though not the precise model that Locke and later Montesquieu developed and that the Americans adopted.[4]

The discussion of the relation of constitutionalism to democracy was complicated by the fact that, both in Europe and America, constitutionalism was at the outset not at all democratic, but rather aristocratic. In spite of the fact that the U.S. Declaration of Independence and the Rights of Man of the French Revolution had proclaimed the equality of all men, dominant political practice remained sceptical.[5] The *Federalist* has not much love for the mass of the common people; it has much to say about the "gusts of popular passion" and the like.[6] Throughout the nineteenth century intellectuals in England and elsewhere were highly critical of democracy.[7] What is more important, in requiring the universal suffrage of men and women; the equal

---

[3] H. R. G. Greaves, *The British Constitution*, 3rd ed., 1955, pp. 20–21, lays the ghost; Karl Löwenstein, *Staatsrecht und Staatspraxis von Grossbritannien*, 1967, Vol. 2, Chapter 9, deals fully with human rights under the British Constitution, as based upon the Bill of Rights of 1688 (1 *Will. 3 and Mary*, sess. 2, c.2) and later enactments. Cf. also the discriminating comments by K. B. Smellie, *Great Britain Since 1688*, 1962, pp. 21 ff.

[4] See above, pp. 18 ff.

[5] See my *Constitutional Government and Democracy*, 1968a, pp. 178 ff. for the party system as a kind of division of power, and Chapter 6, especially pp. 111 ff. for the judiciary.

[6] Giovanni Sartori, "Constitutionalism: A Preliminary Discussion," 1962a and W. H. Morris-Jones, 1965. The argument is reviewed critically above, Chapter 2, note 17.

[7] An able analysis of these writers is given by Benjamin Lippincott, *Victorian Critics of Democracy*, 1938. Macaulay's famous letter to a congressman, as printed in *Harper's Magazine*, Vol. 54, pp. 460 ff., Feb. 1877, should be consulted. We shall have occasion later in the book to refer to some of the many books on democracy. Here mention might be made of my own *The New Belief in the Common Man*, 1941, considerably altered and updated as *Die Demokratie als Herrschaft- und Lebensform*, 2nd ed., 1959, 1966; and to A. D. Lindsay, *The Modern Democratic State*, of which unfortunately only the first volume appeared, 1943; Robert A. Dahl, *A Preface to Democratic Theory*, 1956; William Kornhauser, *The Politics of Mass Society*, 1959; Seymour Martin Lipset, *Political Man*, 1959; Gerhard Leibholz, *Strukturprobleme der modernen Demokratie*, 1958; Giovanni Sartori, *Democratic Theory*, 1962b; Georges Burdeau, *Traité de la Science Politique*, Vol. 5, 1950.

participation of all classes, especially the labor class, in political life; and the elimination of racial and religious discrimination, democracy in the strictest sense spread slowly throughout the nineteenth century, and in fact has not yet reached its culmination.

The milestones in the process of democratizing constitutionalism in the nineteenth century were Jackson's presidency; the Reform Act of 1832; the revolution of 1848 in France; and the Civil War. Although none of these events, obviously, realized democracy, each was a significant forward step. In America, Jackson's presidency provided the first effective frontal attack upon government by the elite; in Britain, through the Reform Act of 1832, and the other great measures of reform that accompanied and followed it, a broad breach was made in the system of government by the privileged, as characterized by "rotten boroughs" and vote restrictions. The revolution of 1848 in France challenged the power of financial and industrial capital, and although its premature, radical experiments with socialism led to the Bonapartist reaction, it nevertheless heralded the coming of labor into its own.

Farther east beyond the Rhine, the revolution of 1848 precipitated an unsuccessful attempt to unite Germany by popular movement, after having swept away the system of Metternich. In Italy a similar initiative failed. But in spite of the fact that popular forces proved too weak to unite and free nations, the idea of self-determination took root. Finally the Civil War in the United States destroyed slavery after four formidable years of armed conflict. In the course of this struggle, the leader of the antislavery forces of the North, Abraham Lincoln, formulated some of the most hallowed tenets of democratic faith. Nowhere has the progressive spirit of democracy found more eloquent expression than in the Gettysburg address: ". . . that government of the people, by the people, for the people shall not perish from the earth." The ideals that inspired that speech are still far from having been realized.

Every one of these milestones marks an element in the process of democratization which in spite of many setbacks is still going forward. In Britain, the successive extensions of the suffrage, eventually embracing women's suffrage, as well as numerous social and governmental reforms, carried on the work that the Reform Act of 1832 began. Likewise in the United States, many administrations in this century have extended and deepened the control over concentrated economic power and monopoly. France, in successive phases of the Third and Fourth Republics, realized part of the program of the revolutionaries of 1848, and in Germany the Weimar Republic gave a first indication of what a fully democratized and socially conscious German people might contribute to a democratic world order. For here, for the first time, *social* democray was taken up in earnest. The Fascist reaction there and in other countries of Europe meant a desperate attempt to stem the tide of advancing democracy. By exploiting all the stresses and strains of a new social pattern, Fascism managed to install itself, and then, by the ruthless employment of every known method of violence, to maintain itself until the inner tensions and strains resulting from such desperate repressive efforts embroiled the Fascist dictators in foreign wars that spelled their doom. But even the dictators found it necessary to make continuous bows toward the people, thus acknowledging the fact that democracy alone nowadays offers legitimacy, an acceptable ground for the exercise of political power.

This increasing recognition of popular majorities as the only basis of legitimate government naturally has led to a fading of the monarchical tradition. Kings, not having been popularly elected, could rarely stand up against a leader of the people. The reign of Queen Victoria is most interesting in this respect. Time and again her monarchical sense of responsibility clashed with the parliamentary responsibility of successive prime ministers. Continental crises may have been more dramatic outwardly; they brought revolution and reaction in their train. But the deep roots that constitutionalism had struck in English thinking make the slow fading of royal prerogative worthy of detailed attention.

The story of the bedchamber comedy is characteristic. Peel would not form a cabinet unless, as evidence of the Queen's confidence, he should be given the right to nominate the ladies of her household. The Queen refused. The Queen thought that she would be "supported by my country who are very enthusiastic about it and loudly cheered me on going to church Sunday." The basis of this conflict was the fact that court gossip still played a significant role in the forming of a government. That was in 1839. It was not long before the idea of the politically "sovereign" people had taken root to such an extent that only the parliamentary support of a man could determine his leadership. The kings and queens just faded out of the picture.[8]

At the present time, it is clear that the contrast between constitutionalist and nonconstitutionalist democracies is of central importance. It is at the heart of what has been miscalled the "cold war" or the "East-West conflict." We say "constitutionalist" rather than "constitutional" in order to highlight the fact that it is the ideology of constitutionalism the presence or absence of which distinguishes these regimes, rather than the presence or absence of a written constitution as such. For the constitution of the Soviet Union may not be a "real" constitution in the Western sense; it may be a facade, and it may fail to guarantee human rights, but its existence cannot be denied. We need to explore at this point in greater depth the other side of the coin and that is the meaning and significance of de-

---

[8] Karl Löwenstein, *Die Monarchie im Modernen Staat*, 1952, has given far and away the most convincing interpretation in contemporary terms.

mocracy. This is no easy task, since democracy is probably the most controversial of the words used in contemporary political discussions.

In 1940, a group of American educators undertook to explore the meaning of democracy, and they found a considerable range of opinion.[9] Among the important "assets" that they thought of as useful in the defense of democracy were, of course, the rights and freedoms of a constitutional order (see Chapter 6 below). Democracy, they said, was both a personal way of life and a system of social and political organization; it is a way of life and a form of rule. They also thought that the political consequence of the moral emphasis of democracy on the worth and dignity of each person is popular sovereignty, in the sense of majority rule. But majority rule is not absolute and does not mean the "tyranny of the majority" which de Tocqueville had identified as the greatest flaw of the American democracy.[10] These educators realized that rights and liberties ought to be protected so that minorities can play their "creative role." Yet one finds no frank admission of the violation of this proposition by the treatment of the American Negro at that time.[11] Their Manifesto concludes with a "creed" consisting of sixty items some of which are patently incompatible with each other. This creed contains an article (45) which holds "that the fundamental civil liberties may not be impaired even by majorities." This means, of course, that these educators accepted constitutional limitations; they cite some of them, such as life and property.[12]

This sort of creed, so confidently stated in 1941 would now, a generation later, encounter serious objections. In a recent publication we read that "the primary question of contemporary democratic theory is, in the end, the question of the proper organization of the revolutionary movement."[13] To be sure, two of the greatest presidents, Thomas Jefferson and Abraham Lincoln, expressed themselves in favor of revolutionary change. Lincoln, in an oft-cited passage of his First Inaugural (March 4, 1861)

[9] "Democracy and Education in the Current Crisis," *Teachers College Record,* November 1940 (also available as separate pamphlet), 101 ff. The "Creed" is found on p. 112 ff.

[10] Alexis de Tocqueville, *Democracy in America,* edited by J. P. Mayer and Max Lerner, in a new translation by George Lawrence, 1966 (Harper & Row), pp. 239–40. (In Philip Bradley's edition, based on Bowen's revision of the Reeve translation, it is found on pp. 269–72).

[11] See e.g. "The Negro in Defense," Nr. 3 of the Council for Democracy's series *Democracy in Action,* 1941. (Herbert J. Seligman drafted this memo on the basis of memoranda furnished by 35 specialists; it was put into final shape by Louis Hartz.)

[12] This creed is found pp. 112–15 of the article cited in note 9 above.

[13] Kenneth A. Megill, *The New Democratic Theory,* 1970, p. 149; a somewhat different line is taken by Harvey Wheeler, *Democracy in a Revolutionary Era,* 1968.

said: "This country with its institutions belongs to the people who in-habit it. Whenever they shall grow weary of existing government, they can exercise their constitutional right of amending it or their revolutionary right to dismember or overthrow it." Jefferson, in a letter, put the propo-sition even more dramatically when he wrote in reference to Shay's Re-bellion: "God forbid we should ever be twenty years without such a rebellion . . . what country can preserve its liberties, if its rulers are not warned from time to time, that the people preserve the spirit of resis-tance. . . . The tree of liberty must be refreshed from time to time with the blood of patriots and tyrants. It is its natural manure. . . ." (letter to Col W. S. Smith, Nov. 13, 1787).

These and similar statements were, of course, in a sense merely echoes of the Declaration of Independence which said ". . . for against despotism, it is their (the citizens') right, it is their duty, to throw off such Government and to provide new Guards for their future security." Note that from the Declaration to Lincoln, a radicalizing of the doctrine by broadening it can be observed. First, it was merely the overthrow of a despotism, such as was in our days attempted by the resistance fighters against Fascism and Naziism. Then it became the maintenance of liberty against "tyrants," and finally, with Lincoln, the justification of a revolution is simply that the people have grown "weary" of the government.

Present-day authors who argue for a revolutionary component of de-mocracy are elaborating this Lincolnian approach, but whereas Lincoln made it clear in his address that only a concern for human rights and democracy could justify such an outlook, now it is a "social order." The author cited at the start of this discussion concludes by proclaiming that a "new era of history has begun." And he details the goal of the revolu-tionary thrust thus: "The new democratic theory is an articulation of this force. The new theory is only beginning to be worked out, but it is already a reality. Hope for a genuinely democratic social order depends upon the success of the movement now being built." [14] Were this true, democracy and totalitarianism would become indistinguishable, for a revolutionary ideology would be characteristic of both. In Rousseau's words: "The gen-eral will is always right." [15] Such a democracy would no longer be con-stitutionalist; it would be absolutist and unlimited.

---

[14] Megill, *New Democratic Theory*, p. 164.

[15] Rousseau's general will has occasioned a great deal of controversy which has not been settled by recent works, such as Judith N. Shklar's *Men and Citizens*, 1969; Guy H. Dodge, ed., *Jean-Jacques Rousseau: Authoritarian Libertarian?*, 1971; John W. Chapman, *Rousseau—Totalitarian or Liberal?*, 1956. Cf. also Raymond Polin, *La Politique de la Solitude*, 1971 (Paris: Sirey), Chapter 4, 2. See for the many formulations of the doctrine by Rousseau my *Inevitable Peace*, 1948, Chapter 6. It is not the will of the majority, as Rousseau himself states quite explicitly, yet one finds the general will by counting votes. Cf. *Contrat Social*, Book 4, Chapter 2.

This argument goes back to the early years of the American republic; it is not new to the nineteenth century, as many believe. Robert A. Dahl has, in his study of democracy, juxtaposed Madisonian and populist democracy. Madisonian democracy is constitutionalist democracy, beset by the inherent contradiction between the majority principle and constitutionalist limitations. The populist view eliminates all restrictions and with de Tocqueville, makes "the very essence of democratic government," "the absolute sovereignty of the majority." [16] On the basis of such a juxtaposition of traditional views, Dahl develops the notion of a polyarchal democracy which is a hybrid of the two types. But whether hybrid or not, it still involves the contradiction between the preferences of the majority and constitutional limitations. To make these limitations themselves a matter of majority preference is a refinement of the problem; it does not alter its basic structure.

In order to progress with the analysis, it appears necessary to analyze with greater care the meaning of "majority will" or whatever other expression is used to designate the preference of the larger number of participants in a political order. Dahl states at the outset three conditions: (1) every member of the organization expresses his preference for one of the alternatives, for example by voting; (2) these expressions are treated as identical in weight; (3) the alternative with the greatest number of preferences is the winner.[17] To these conditions he adds in the course of his analysis three more, namely, (4) members may add an alternative not previously identified; (5) all members possess identical information about the alternatives; (6) the preferred alternatives become operational and are executed by those in authority. Dahl adds that "no human organization has ever met or is ever likely to meet these conditions."

The problem then becomes: what are the necessary and sufficient conditions in the real world for the existence of these six conditions to a minimum degree that constitute polyarchy? Since the information needed to answer this question is neither available nor likely to become so soon, Dahl proceeds to transform his six conditions into rules in which the existence of consensus becomes determining. Polyarchy, therefore, is a function of consensus on the six norms; it varies in the degree of its realization in accordance with the degree of consensus on the several conditions. But "by their propensity for political passivity the poor and uneducated disfranchise themselves." And "anything like equal control over governmental policy is triply barred to the members of Madison's unpropertied masses.

---

[16] Alexis de Tocqueville, *Democracy in America*, as cited above, Chapter 4, note 10.

[17] Robert A. Dahl, *A Preface to Democratic Theory*, 1956, Chapter 3—somewhat simplified by me.

They are barred by their relatively greater inactivity, by their relatively limited access to resources, and by Madison's nicely contrived system of constitutional checks." [18]

How then are we to resolve the contradiction just stated? Purely formally, it could be done by making the majority the determining factor deciding such limitations. It is unrealistic and contrary to fact to assert that a bare majority has unlimited power in a democracy. It is worse to define democracy in such terms, because such a view neglects the actual workings of democratic institutions and, if adopted, would jeopardize their successful maintenance. The public, in America and elsewhere, has rarely adopted the rigid majoritarian position. Going by common sense rather than theory, men feel the confusion of the abstract "either-or" which contrasts majority rule with minority rule. The public is for majority rule, to be sure, but it perceives the need for flexibility in determining what shall constitute a majority. It is, on the whole, less obvlivious than the political partisan to the fact that a working scheme of cooperation among men of different views and interests calls for a sense of mutual give and take.

The vital issue as to whose views shall prevail in a democracy, and whose views *do* prevail in a democracy, has never been very clearly analyzed by the political theorists. In the thirties the issue was much beclouded by the bitter controversy over the role of the courts in the American past and future. [19] Majority rule was in that context usually identified with congressional majorities or presidential programs, and contrasted with minority rule, epitomized by the "nine old men." [20]

More recently, the partisanship has been reversed. The "Warren Court" became the friend of progressive forces which left the problem unresolved of who was more democratic. The rule of law versus the rule of politicians was the battle cry. Who, being a believer in constitutionalism, can be in doubt if the issue is raised in such terms? [21] And yet it has been insisted that there is a limitation on the power of the existing majority: the principle of majority rule itself. For this principle "guarantees the eternal right of the individual and the minority to work openly at all times

---

[18] Dahl, *Preface to Democratic Theory*, p. 81; see also Peter Bachrach, and Morton Baratz, *Power and Poverty*, 1970, who stress that the deep-seated grievances of the poor make them "troublesome in the participatory process."

[19] See, e.g., Max Lerner's able but one-sided statement in "Minority Rule and the Constitutional Tradition" in C. Read, ed., *The Constitution Reconsidered*, 1938, pp. 191 ff.

[20] See, e.g., Edwin Mims, Jr., *The Majority of the People: A Grammar of Democracy*, 1941.

[21] See, e.g., McIlwain's thoughtful, but also one-sided, statement in "The Fundamental Law Behind the Constitution of the United States," in *The Constitution Reconsidered*, 1938, pp. 33 ff.

toward the formation of a new majority." [22] The attempt to identify majority rule with totalitarian dictatorship is mistaken. The problem is what is the democratic balance between majority and minority. This balance may be stated in terms of rights, or of powers, or of rule; whichever the frame of reference, it is a question of balance rather than a clear-cut alternative between majority and minority.

What constitutes a majority? The extreme majoritarian view has been stated with trenchant emphasis as follows: "In any decision-making group one half of the members, plus one, have a *right* to commit one half of the members, minus one, to any policy they see fit to support." [23] This principle the author of the statement claims as the essence of democratic government. The advantage of this flat statement of the majoritarian position is that it avoids all subterfuges. It is set forth as the acme of radical progressivism.

In my opinion, the flat majoritarian position represents a common error made by many progressives, and it is in the interest of a progressive majority that it should be opposed. Modern democracy urgently requires our abandoning this abstract, mathematical view of the problem of majority rule. There are three crucial unexplained major premises involved: (1) that there is no difference in importance between "policies," though such a difference is implied in the American tradition of constitutional versus ordinary legislation; (2) that a majority will necessarily respect the minority's right openly to attempt to form a new majority; (3) that policies are merely matters of willful "decision," that is to say, that there is no difference between policies which can, and policies which cannot, be enforced.

All three of these assumptions are untenable. To begin with the last, statute books are littered with enactments that are dead letters because they are unenforceable. You cannot enforce a statute "to maintain competition" when the economic factors make for monopoly. The minority opposed to such a statute is going to prevail, not because its "will" is superior, but because its insight is, for nature's laws are always enforced. One of the most common failings of majorities, particularly when they are compounded of diverse groups, is to enact statutes with mutually exclusive objectives. Such statutes can never be enforced intact, and the majority's will is to that extent nullified.

Second, there is, unfortunately, plenty of evidence to show that on many occasions the majority will not respect the minority's right to build a majority. Indeed, this right has to be hedged about by numerous constitutional safeguards protecting the freedom of expression. Freedom of speech,

---

[22] Mims, *Majority of the People,* p. 33.

[23] Willmore Kendall, "The Majority Principle and the Scientific Elite," 1939.

of the press, and of peaceful assembly are continuously imperiled by the majority's inclination to deny the minority's right to build a majority. An examination of the records of the Civil Liberties Union during the last twenty-five years will destroy any illusions on that score. Many of these rights, even though constitutionally guaranteed, are continually being curtailed by the majority's pressure, even to the point of violence. The mere fact that the minority is *supposed* to be protected by constitutional safeguards constitutes no actual protection.

Finally, would any man seriously question that there is considerable difference in the importance of popular decisions—that, for instance, it is one thing to decide to increase the income tax, and quite another to curtail freedom of speech? Since the radical majoritarians are in the habit of citing Rousseau, they may be reminded that Rousseau sharply differentiated between the majorities required for different kinds of decisions. This is important, because Rousseau left little doubt that democracy was his ideal. He stood ready to accept the judgment of the common man without equivocation or resource to a "higher law." Yet how did Rousseau feel on the subject of majorities? "The vote of the majority always binds the rest." Does Rousseau mean by a majority a majority of one? Here is what he writes:

> There are two general rules that may serve to regulate the relation between voting and the general will. First, the more grave and important the questions discussed, the nearer should the opinion that is to prevail approach to unanimity. Second, the more the matter in hand calls for speed, the smaller the prescribed difference in the number of votes may be allowed to become: where an instant decision has to be reached, a majority of one should be enough. The first of these two rules seems more in harmony with the laws, and the second with practical affairs. In any case, it is the combination of them that gives the best proportions for determining the majority necessary.[24]

According to Rousseau, a majority of one suffices only in the case of the need of an instant decision. It is restricted to outright emergencies. Democratic practice has become less cautious; simple pluralities are accepted for many "grave and important questions," general laws of far-reaching consequence.

The constituent power—that is to say, the residuary power of the people "to reform, alter, or abolish" the government—stems from the great constitutional struggle that rent England during the seventeenth century. The idea has medieval roots, and it was persuasively stated by John Locke

---

[24] *Social Contract,* Book 4, Chapter 2.

after the Glorious Revolution. It was repeatedly and flatly set forth by the makers of the American Constitution, more especially James Wilson, Sam Adams, and George Mason. The term "constituent power" was central in the political thought of John Adams.

All this is very well known. But it is equally true that throughout this body of thinking there is a lack of precision when it comes to explaining just what this constituent power consists of. When these writers speak of "the people," whom do they mean? A majority of one? Since the decision concerning the form of government is certainly a grave and important one, we may suspect that they do not. We cannot escape from this issue by constitutional provisions for an amending power. No matter how elaborate the provisions for an amending power may be, they should not from a political viewpoint, be assumed to have superseded the constituent power, for the constituent power is the power that made the Constitution. It remains in the people, who are not bound by their ancestors to any existing governmental pattern. It is the power to make a revolution. We say "power" deliberately, rather than "right." For it is a purely factual, norm-creating thing, this power to establish a constitution or a pattern of government. What more can be said about it?

The constituent power is exercised by the constituent group. The constituent group can come into operation only when the government fails to function constitutionally, i.e., becomes arbitrary and tyrannical. Its function results from the residuary and unorganized power of resistance in the community. The constituent group is neither a class nor any other established sector of the community; it forms spontaneously in response to the need of the revolutionary situation. The more intelligent and vital members of the community are apt to take things into their own hands when the situation becomes serious; for these men have a natural desire for freedom. Arbitrary power will not long be endured by them.

But the traditional doctrine of the seventeenth and eighteenth centuries, the doctrine as we find it in Locke as well as in revolutionary America, has two important defects—defects which have tended to discredit it in the past. These two defects are (1) that the doctrine failed to make it explicit that the constituent group as defined can come into play *only* against arbitrary power, but not against a functioning constitutionalism, and (2) that the doctrine fails to emphasize the specific function of the constituent group, namely, to build a constitution.

The two defects are clearly corollaries, for there is not likely to be any widespread demand for a new constitution so long as the existing constitution functions effectively. Under such conditions, the demand for a new constitution would not receive sufficient support, nor could the building of such a constitution count upon general approval. Yet there may be widespread disagreement as to whether an existing constitution is functioning satisfactorily. Millions of unemployed are likely to take a view of present-day constitutionalism in America different from that of more successful groups in the community. In the last analysis, the community itself is the judge, according to the doctrine of the constituent power.

Before the advent of the New Deal, disagreement became so sharp in the thirties that a revolutionary situation threatened. But no constituent group arose in America. Instead the policies of the Roosevelt administration convinced the people that there were as yet great resources within the existing framework of government, and so the revolutionary impulse subsided. Far from being the dictator that his opponents accused him of being, Roosevelt was, in fact, the savior of constitutionalism. He proved that it still was a functioning system in this country. The common man's judgment was definitely that American constitutionalism was not tyrannical and arbitrary. This is important, because democratic constitutionalism is directed against the establishment of such arbitrary power; conversely, only the general conviction that such arbitrary power has arisen calls forth a constituent group and revolutionary action.

But if such a group forms and revolutionary action takes place, it is constituent only if the group undertakes to set up a new constitution. The fact that the constituent group possesses its power for the purpose of setting up a new constitution makes it inadmissible to call this group the sovereign. A constitutional democracy has no sovereign, but it recognizes a constituent power, a residuary power of the community behind and beyond all government capable of destroying the existing constitution and establishing a new one.

This recognition of the ultimate popular sanction of the constitution itself depends upon the belief in the common man. This belief at the same time clearly implies the recognition of the constituent power. But not every revolutionary power is a constituent power, even if it is a majority. No constituent power was exercised by any constituent group in Germany when Hitler became dictator. It was an anti-constitutional reaction. The same holds true of the two Napoleons.

Rousseau buttressed the idea of a qualified majority for grave and important questions by his famous doctrine of the "real constitution." This he considered the most important of all kinds of law. It "is not graven on tablets of marble or brass, but on the hearts of the citizens." Rousseau is here referring to morality, custom, and public opinion. In his day, Rousseau could claim, though not quite justly, that these factors were unknown to political thinkers. Since his time, their role has come to be increasingly recognized. We know morality, custom, and particularly public opinion to be continuously evolving. There can be little question that the rise of modern propaganda and of the mass media force us to modify Rousseau's views concerning the "real constitution."

In giving up the notion of a "real constitution," do we have to sur-render the idea of qualified majorities with it? Far from it. The argument for qualified majorities rests upon considerations of political prudence. In an environment shot through with propaganda of all kinds, the common man's ability to think a matter out for himself requires more time if the matter is of great weight. The common man is neither infallible nor super-human in virtue. His quality of judgment and character results from a vivid sense of values. That fact is the basis for a belief in the qualified majority.

If very deep-seated feelings are involved in a decision, even though only the feelings of a substantial minority, democratic government will hesitate to go forward upon the basis of a bare majority preference. A good constitution will demark clearly what are grave and more important decisions. Obviously the gravest issue is the making of the constitution as a whole; the next most important is any alteration in its specific provi-sions. In England, where there is no single constitutional document, seri-ous issues are continuously dubbed constitutional, and there is no more effective argument against any policy than that it raises a "constitutional question." There is an implied suggestion here that the issue at hand should be submitted to the voter in a general election. To be sure, a mere plurality would, in fact, decide the matter if an election were held. But a detailed study of English practice reveals a hesitancy to proceed unless the ma-jority is "substantial." [25] In any event, a general election consumes much time and money, and thereby provides an opportunity for a threatened minority to organize effective resistance.

These arguments are reinforced by a very practical consideration: the marginal or "floating" voters. The relatively few who pass from one side to the other, and thereby spell victory or defeat for the government, keep the government majority alert to any substantial minority view. The complete disregard of any such minority is rather improbable. This does not, of course, apply to the extremists on the opposite side; e.g., the Con-servatives may safely disregard the Communists, and Labour the Diehard Tories. But they must respect their own extremists, as well as all the marginal groups who may go over to the other camp.

A country so closely knit and so definitely held together by its com-mon heritage as England may discard the safeguard of qualified majorities; yet its example may not be a safe one for less fortunate communities to follow. The fact is that English political tradition has evolved restraints upon the majority that are not available elsewhere. In the United States, qualified majorities are an integral part of constitutional provisions. Be-sides the enlarged majorities required for an amendment of the federal

[25] Cf. for a splendid exposition of this kind of democratic group pluralism, Eduard Heimann, *Communism, Fascism, or Democracy?*, 1938, especially pp. 267 ff.

Constitution, similar provisions are found in many of the state constitutions. In Europe, qualified majority requirements are quite common in constitutional provisions for amendment, usually two-thirds or even three-fourths being required. At times, instead of such a qualification, there is a time qualification, that is to say, after a certain lapse of time, the provision has to be reenacted, before it becomes law.

Against all such provisions, the argument is advanced that they give too much power to a minority. Obviously, as a result of such provisions, a minority can veto the majority's will. That would clearly appear to be undemocratic, if the majority-of-one principle is considered the quintessence of democracy. It has been shown that this view is mistaken. But let us be more concrete and realistic and face the question: does the requirement of a qualified majority mean entrenching the present vested interests of our economy and protecting them against the majority will? This has been cogently argued time and again. It is, however, in the light of experience an overstatement of a palpable fact. To say that a qualified majority delays changes is almost tautological; if it didn't, what would be the purpose of having it? To say that a qualified majority prevents changes is largely untrue; if it did, the United States would have neither an income tax nor woman suffrage, nor the extension of the suffrage to eighteen-year-olds.

The usual argument about minority rule amounts to a play with the word "rule." The mere fact that certain actions can be prevented by a determined minority does not make that minority the ruler, even though it gives it a strong share in the rule. No one has yet been able to say how minorities can be adequately protected under a constitution without granting them such constitutional safeguards as will enable them to participate in ruling through their power of resistance.

Let us accept, then, the proposition that qualified majorities are in keeping with the basic principle of majority rule, indeed that such qualifications frequently are the direct outgrowth of the majority principle itself. The only question that remains is: How shall they be qualified? It seems to many that our own amending process is too cumbersome. I share this view. I believe that the greatest service a political party could render to political improvement in this country would be to amend the amending clause so as to provide for a cheaper and swifter process. Certainly Switzerland has prospered under a much simpler plan; the same is true of many of our state constitutions.

It is, by definition, impossible to lay down rules as to the majorities required for revolutionary alterations of a constitution. It is apparent from what has been said, however, that the majorities required would probably be sizable, at least in the initial stages. The problem is largely of an academic nature, since it is the experience of working constitutional systems to obliterate the need for such upheavals by yielding to the demand for changes, no matter how basic. There is, for example, little question that the government of the United States has developed into what some like to refer to as a "service state," others as a "welfare state," still others as "socialism." What all these words seek to indicate is the undeniable growth of numerous regulatory and service functions which the American government did not exercise a hundred years ago. There is, furthermore, reason to believe that the American government will continue to develop in whatever directions seem desirable to the people at large. Insofar as these developments are successful adaptations to a changed economic environment, they vindicate our belief in democratic constitutionalism.

What is so easily forgotten by those who chafe under the restraints that hinder them in doing the seemingly right thing is that in a democracy they are committed to carrying the rest of the community with them. Nothing, in other words, is intrinsically right unless and until it is approved by suitable majorities. This does not mean that what majorities approve is therefore right—far from it. Majorities are not infallible, any more than are the common men who compose them. Safeguards are needed. If by such safeguards self-interested minorities can entrench themselves and thwart the realization of the majority's interest for any length of time, then steps can and usually will be taken to defeat such self-interested minorities.

The protection of minorities as such cannot be surrendered as a principle because of such possibilities. Labor has least reason to espouse the doctrine of the extreme majoritarians. This needs to be stated emphatically, since quite a few men who consider themselves the special friends of the workers have enunciated such extreme views. Karl Marx insisted that the workers were bound to become the majority and could then go forward to realize socialism or communism. The fact is, however, that even now, a hundred years after Marx's analysis, the workers do not command a majority in any country, nor do they show any sign of commanding one in the foreseeable future. This is the conclusive reason for their interest in constitutional protection of minority rights, for the chances are considerably greater that "big business" may bring together a bare majority for a short time with the aid of a demagogue. The experience in various European countries, and especially in Germany, should go a long way toward proving that no greater disaster can befall the workers than that rigidly majoritarian views should prevail at such a time. Even at the risk of considerably delaying what they consider necessary social gains, labor is more vitally concerned than any other group in the maintenance of constitutional democracy.

A leading theorist of markedly progressive views has recently written: "No majority, unless it abrogates democracy, can decide to kill the members of the minority . . . to repeal the rights of national or religious groups, or to prohibit the free and dignified expression of independent and possibly non-conformist opinions. It is only within certain constitutional limits that a majority can act and that a change in the majority . . . may affect the course of policy." [26] Although a bit extreme, this view focuses attention upon the fact that the process of protecting the minority in opposition to the majority is part of the concept of majority rule itself.

In conclusion, it can be said that majority rule is indeed the quintessence of democracy, if it is not taken to mean "majority-of-one." Such majority rule does not conflict with constitutionalism, understood as limiting the exercise of power and rule even of the people, if these limits are themselves adopted by a majority of the people. Since a change in such limits may constitute a revolution, to that extent a democratic constitution has revolutionary potentials built into it. Should revolution, however, be more narrowly understood to involve violence, as Jefferson's remark about the blood of patriots would appear to imply, then revolutionary activity is excluded; for alterations adopted by majority vote live up to the long-standing injunction of substituting ballots for bullets.

[26] Heimann, *Communism, Fascism, or Democracy?*, p. 279.

FEDERAL
CONSTITUTIONAL-
ISM

5

The rise of modern constitutional government has been accompanied by the establishment of an increasing number of federal schemes. The parallel is so striking that federalism may be considered one of the most important aspects of constitutionalism.[1] Federalism, when spoken of in general discussions, is used rather vaguely to mean any kind of association of autonomous units. The word may therefore refer to a league or federation of states, as well as to a federal system, such as that of the United States. Not only this country, but Switzerland, Germany, Canada, Australia, the Union of South Africa, Brazil, Austria, India, Nigeria, Malaysia, and others have evolved a governmental structure of the federal type. The organization of the world at large into the United Nations points in the same direction, and so does a united Europe, though both are at present loose leagues or federations of states. Many of the more close-knit federal systems developed their structures out of a preceding league.

The following discussion will not be concerned with controversies about "sovereignty" and the "state," or where one finds sovereignty in federal systems. Instead, it will discuss federalism as a process providing a territorial form of dividing political powers under a constitution. A great many of the arguments and controversies over whether a particular political order is federal or confederal result from precisely this neglect of process as contrasted with structure. They have bedeviled the politics of Euopean unification. They are now troubling other federalizing processes, including those in Africa, the Caribbean, and the world at large. The real

---

[1] K. C. Wheare, *Federal Government,* 3rd ed., 1953, Chapter 3; it should be noted that Wheare writes of federal *government,* and not of federalism. Cf. my more recent *Trends of Federalism in Theory and Practice,* 1968b, and the literature cited there, especially Arthur Maass, ed., *Area and Power,* 1959.

problem, politically, is whether the federalizing process is in progress and whether the institutional structure as it evolves facilitates the changes required by it.

Federal schemes, generally speaking, seek to combine a measure of unity with a measure of diversity; usually the diversity follows a territorial pattern, such as French spoken in western Switzerland, German in eastern Switzerland.[2] Federalism is the form of political organization suited to communities where this territorially-diversified pattern of values, interests, beliefs, and traditions can be effectively implemented by joint efforts in the pursuit of common values and interests and by the cultivation of common beliefs and traditions. Whether the particular federal structure is best described as a single federal government or as a federation of several governments may sometimes be difficult to determine.

When the particularistic local objectives are sufficiently strong and compact to hold together the territorial subdivisions of the more comprehensive group, sustaining them as or molding them into autonomous groups, then the adequate political pattern is federational. On the other hand, the federal organization comes into existence when conflicting objectives (interests, traditions, values) are not as yet, or are no longer, sufficiently strong to sustain autonomous units. The contrast between the federal and the federational type of organization must not blind us, therefore, to the great similarities between them. Communities pass readily from one into the other. For federalism may be seen as a dynamic process, and not merely as a static design.[3] Any particular design or pattern of competencies or jurisdictions is a phase, a short-run state of a continually evolving political reality. This fact has only in recent years become recognized. A sketch, even in outline, of this evolution of federal theory is a rather complicated affair.[4]

Earlier thought down to the end of the eighteenth century was preoccupied with the problem of how to safeguard the component units of a federal system against encroachments, and it stressed the contractual nature of the federal bond. The great turn comes with the *Federalist* and

---

[2] E.g., Chapter 6 (A. E. Sutherland), Chapter 4 (Bowie), Chapter 9 (Brinser), and Chapter 10 (Friedrich and Mavrinac), concerned respectively with commerce and transportation, defense, agriculture and labor, in Robert R. Bowie and Carl J. Friedrich, eds., *Studies in Federalism*, 1954, dealing with Australia, Canada, Germany, the United States, and Switzerland on a comparative basis.

[3] The following discussion is taken from my paper, "Federalism, National and International in Theory and Practice," read before the Oxford Round Table Meeting of the International Political Science Association in 1963a.

[4] See for this my article "Origin and Development of the Concept of Federalism in the United States," in *Jahrbuch des öffentlichen Rechts der Gegenwart*, Neue Folge, Band 9, pp. 29 ff.

the innovations hammered out at the convention in Philadelphia; there, and from then on, the preoccupation of the theory of federalism is with how to organize an effective unity and thereby allow a federal order to become a "state." The theory presented in the *Federalist* embodies the successful surmounting of the practical difficulties and the beginning of modern federal theory.

"Federalism" seems the most suitable term by which to designate the process of federalizing a political grouping, that is to say, the process by which a number of separate political organizations, be they states or any other kind of associations, enter into arrangements for working out solutions, adopting joint policies, and making joint decisions on joint problems; or, reversely, the process through which a hitherto unitary political community, as it becomes differentiated into a number of separate and distinct political communities, achieves a new organization in which the differentiated communities, now separately organized, become capable of working out separately and on their own those problems they no longer have in common. But it is not only a matter of decision-making, but of the entire range of power and its exercise. The federalizing process accompanies, so to speak, the communal development as its organizational counterpart. If values, interests, and beliefs exhibit a stable and structured pattern in which the commonly shared values, interests, and beliefs are counterbalanced by values, interests, and beliefs that are not shared, though territorially distributed, then a federal development becomes possible. Take, for example, trade unions, which have formed extensive federations in all industrialized countries, such as the American Federation of Labor and the British Trade Union Congress. Each competent unit at first had its own interest, associated with distinctive values and beliefs. But these unions soon discovered that they shared not only values and beliefs, but also broader common interests. Federation then was indicated and was not slow in coming, challenging and eventually eliciting the organizing ability of the leaders of the component units. The same holds true for churches and many other groups. Whenever such groups cannot, or rather do not, wish to merge, because of their distinctive values and beliefs, their self and identity, yet need to unite for the accomplishment of common objectives, usually springing from common needs, federation is indicated. It is essentially the fact that unity is combined with diversity in such a fashion that there coexist spheres of autonomy for the inclusive and the exclusive community, that there coexist spheres of loyalty for both, and that a distinctive characteristic, whether it be living in a particular territory, belonging to a particular church, or practicing a particular trade, can be made the basis of assigning persons to the exclusive as well as the inclusive communities.

The federalizing process may indeed commence in the forming of a league, such as the Council of Europe, the North Atlantic Community, or the confederation that preceded the forming of the United States of America. Or it may lead to such loose association as that of the British Commonwealth of Nations. But always there is the problem of how to combine local autonomy with comprehensive unity.

In short, we can properly speak of federalism only if a set of political groupings coexist and interact as automonous entities, united in a common order with an autonomy of its own.[5]

FEDERALISM AND DEMOCRACY
The relation of the federalizing process to the functioning of democracy is of great importance. If democracy is understood in terms of the absolute and unrestrained rule of the majority of the members of a given political community, then a stark and unresolved conflict between federalism and democracy must be acknowledged.[6] Absolutist democracy is incompatible with federalism, because it does not permit an effective division of power. This aspect probably explains in part the general penchant of radical democrats all over Europe, such as the British Labour Party, to be wary of European federalism. For there can be little doubt that the "sovereign will" of the British electorate might be thwarted if it has to adjust to what other European electorates prefer or reject. More specifically, socialism may become more difficult of achievement if it has to be worked out on a European plane.

These difficulties can be resolved if one is willing to accept a constitutional as opposed to an absolutist democracy. All that is then required is to recognize that every member of the inclusive political order is part of, that is to say, a citizen of, two communities operating on two levels, the regional and the national (federal). A given group of persons, A1, A2, A3, . . . , and another group B1, B2, B3, . . . , "belong" not only to community A or community B, but also to community AB, which includes them both and is therefore a composite community. The participating decisions of these persons, their "will" in the old-fashioned terminology, shape communal action through effective participation in the communal decisions of AB as well as either A or B. The inclusive community as well as the included community being politically organized, democracy, far from clashing with federalism, now is seen to *require* it whenever a composite community exhibits more than one level of effective communal existence in terms of distinctive values, interests, and beliefs.

---

[5] Cf. my *Man and His Government*, 1963b, Chapter 30, as well as Bowie and Friedrich, *Studies in Federalism*, Introduction.

[6] For a pointed statement of this view, representative of the outlook of many "radical" democrats found among European socialists, cf. Franz L. Neumann, "Federalism and Freedom: A Critique" in Arthur W. MacMahon, ed., *Federalism: Mature and Emergent*, 1955, pp. 44–55.

Federalism also tends to impinge on party structures.[7] The comparative analysis of party systems has highlighted the fact that in federal regimes parties tend toward paralleling the government setup. American parties are seen essentially as federations of state parties; similar trends may be observed in other federally organized countries. Political science has recognized for some time that the organizational structure of parties tends to correspond to the governmental pattern under constitutional democracy. This is only natural, since it is one of the purposes of parties to gain control of the government; therefore, if the government is federally structured, parties must adapt themselves to such a structure. In Germany and Switzerland, there is stronger cohesion in the national party organizations than in the United States, corresponding to the tighter federalism in these countries. But the Land and Canton parties display a much greater degree of autonomy than do party subdivisions in unitary such as England.

The interaction between governmental structure and party organization is also to be observed in authoritarian regimes based upon a single party. Only here it is the government that responds to the centralizing impact of the party. Notably in the Soviet Union the formal federalism of the governmental structure is superseded and transcended by the integrating force of the CPSU. This does not mean, as is often asserted, that the federal system has no significance in the Soviet Union; it is, as indicated before, a formalized system of decentralization. But it cannot resist the centralizing impact of the single party. For this to happen, there would have to be at least two parties so that in some of the component units the "other party" than the one being in power at the center could render effective the local autonomy under some such slogan as states' rights. Even so, deep-rooted local differentiation may reinforce the local party organization, as was the case, for example, in the Ukraine and in Georgia, which have long traditions of resistance to central Russian predominance.[8]

Federal legislative assemblies present some interesting general problems. Typically, they are composed of two chambers, one of which represents the people at large, the other the states. Owing to the variety of possible origins, every federalism is likely to be different from every other. The wealth of heterogeneous forms in the composition of federal representative assemblies may well startle the student. The distribution of their legislative functions is even more complex. Many federal constitutions contain long catalogues of what the federal legislature may do; the American Constitution is relatively simple as compared to the German Basic Law. It goes without saying that such divisions of the "competencies," that is,

[7] For the following discussion, see my *Trends of Federalism in Theory and Practice,* 1968b.

[8] Klaus von Beyme, "Federal Theory and Party Reality in the Soviet Union," 1964.

the sphere within which each may operate, must and will vary according to time and space. Economic and social life and the military and geographical factors all will play their role in determining the particular arrangement.

From a political standpoint, no distinctive generalization of principles can be derived. It is a question of more or less; if the functions of the central government are increasing at the expense of those of the local governments, the federal government may become dominant. Jurists have stressed the difference between a central government with powers specifically delegated to it, such as those of the United States, Switzerland, and Germany, and one in which the powers are specifically delegated to the provinces, as in the case of Canada. The existence of residuary powers has been held to constitute the decisive test of "statehood" for the component units. In reality, such residuary powers are an illusion if the powers or functions delegated to the central government are practically all-embracing, as they were in Weimar Germany; broad delegated powers would mean more "local government" in actual practice than such a "residue" of "genuine self-determination." In either case, the only guaranty for whatever distribution of functions there is, delegated or residuary, is the constitution that determines the governmental structure as a whole.

In sum, a comparison of the several federal constitutions shows that certain matters, such as foreign affairs, customs, money and currency, posts, and national defense, are invariably attributed to the federal authorities. On the other hand, certain matters, such as education and cultural affairs, the police, and local government, are usually left to the component units. But the focal point of modern life, namely, the economy in all its ramifications of technology, welfare, and taxation, is handled with the widest variation. Whether by judicial interpretation of the commerce clause, or by amendments broadening the scope of federal jurisdiction, we find that the United States, Switzerland, and all the other federal systems display the most varied distribution of functions and competencies.

The second organizational feature of a federation is the federal division of the executive-administrative sphere (see also Chapter 8 below.) The local units as such have a part either in selecting the federal executive or in conducting the executive work for the whole, or both. The federal structures in the United States, Switzerland, Germany, and the Dominions all satisfy this criterion. To be sure, in none of them (except the German Empire) have the local units more than fragments of the power of selecting the federal executive. Thus, in the United States we may say that voting by states in the electoral college is a partial recognition of the states; for the president is not elected by a majority of the whole people, but by a majority of state majorities. Another fragment of state participation is the constitutional right of the American Senate to advise on and consent to presidential appointments. Out of this has grown the rather important tradition of "senatorial courtesy." It is a kind of *liberum veto,* and means no more than this: that while the Senate will not suggest particular nominations, it expects that the president, in naming certain local officeholders, will choose persons satisfactory to the senator or senators of the president's political party from the state in which the officers are located, or from which the appointees come.

In Switzerland, the members of the executive are elected by the two houses of the legislature; hence the cantons have a decisive voice. The strength of local autonomy is recognized in certain customs: Bern and Zürich are always represented in the executive, and seats are evenly distributed among the other cantons. This means primarily that the French and Italian cantons get at least one or two members. The executive councillors elect the president from among themselves for one year.

Under the Basic Law of the Federal Republic, the federal element is formally weak in the executive sphere. To be sure, state legislatures are given a share in the election of the president, but he is largely a figurehead. The chancellor is appointed by him on recommendation of the majority of the *Bundestag* without any references to the Federal Council. But the reality of politics provides a somewhat greater scope to federalizing tendencies, largely as a result of the federal structure of German political parties. The position of a leader like Franz Josef Strauss rests basically upon his local Bavarian following.

All in all, in many ways the most crucial task to solve, if the forming of a league is to initiate a progressive federalizing process, appears to be the establishment of a workable joint executive. It was so understood in the setting up of the European Coal and Steel Community and of the Common Market; its absence has frustrated the Council of Europe. Historical evidence in support of this general proposition is abundant. This is not to say that the creation of such an executive establishment guarantees the forward march of the federalizing process; obstacles to such a development, that is to say, divisive forces, may be too strong for real progress. The history of the United Nations to date amply corroborates this conclusion.[9] But for all federal systems in their early stages the executive is crucial, because rule-making is restricted to the making of the original treaty and its amendment. In the selection of the executive, the stage of federalizing will be reflected: the further developed in the direction of a unity a political order is, the more completely will the executive be a functionary of the inclusive community and its representatives.

Federalism may also be viewed as a pattern of opposition.[10] From this vantage point the following hypotheses would apply: Federalism (1)

---

[9] See Jean Siotis, *Essai sur le Secrétariat International,* 1963, and Inis L. Claude, *Swords Into Plowshares,* rev. ed., 1959, especially Chapter 10.

[10] See Chapter 7 in my *Trends of Federalism,* footnote 7.

increases the opportunities for dissenting minorities to make their views known to other citizens and policy makers; (2) multiplies the opportunities for citizens to participate in political life; (3) enhances consensus in political discussion in the sense that solutions are sought that will reduce the size, resentments, and coercion of defeated minorities; (4) greatly improves the chances of the peaceful resolution of conflicts; (5) aids the solving of urgent policy questions by providing an opportunity for experimenting with solutions on a limited scale; and (6) enhances confidence in and loyalty to a constitutional polity.[11]

Federalism is particularly fascinating with regard to temporary opposition. By temporary opposition I mean one which is carried forward by men who consider themselves an integral part of the general constituency and therefore expect to become the government, that is, to convert their minority following into a majority. It is an opposition whose values, interests, and beliefs may well become those of the majority of the population. Such an opposition is dynamic rather than static; in opposing, it strives to change the political situation so as to enable it to govern rather than oppose.

A dynamic opposition will therefore marshal all the resources of persuasion and propaganda for the achievement of its central goal. A federal system greatly enhances its chance of doing so. For by becoming first the government in one state, *Land*, or canton, it achieves the authority and secures for itself the resources and tactical advantages which a government naturally possesses. Party history in the United States provides many interesting examples for this federally conditioned rise of oppositional elements, especially within parties. The radical progressivism of midwestern republicanism in the era of Senator LaFollette is the most striking illustration, but the so-called Bull Moose movement of Theodore Roosevelt is another one. The New Deal of Franklin Roosevelt for example, had its experimental beginnings in his governorship of New York State. Earlier the Bull Moose movement of Theodore Roosevelt began as a regional phenomenon.

The dangerous potential of this kind of local experimentation lies in the opportunities a federal order provides for destructive movements of opposition to install themselves and thus achieve an operating base. Here the most famous instance is provided by the history of the German National Socialist movement. The conquest of Thuringia and other small *Länder* gave the Hitler movement the chance to "prove" its capacity to participate in German government. A special feature was the chance it offered the Nazis to naturalize Hitler; without that he could not have become Chan-

---

[11] Cf. the statement in Robert A. Dahl, *Political Opposition in Western Democracies*, 1966.

cellor. It is, however, possible that in mature democratic societies, this danger could be minimized by providing, as does the American constitution (Article IV, 4) that the component units must maintain a constitutional democratic order. Thus opposition would be restricted to parties and formations that do not attack the basic principles of the popular consensus.[12]

Federalism requires relative stability in the executive. It has for some time been argued that a federal regime is hard to combine with a parliamentary executive of the British cabinet type. It is so combined in Canada, Australia, and the German Federal Republic, but considerable difficulties result from the fact that the relation between the opposition and the government is thereby given a chance of erupting into an electoral struggle. For under conditions of parliamentary dependency of the cabinet, elections may be called on the national as well as the local level at any time, and the resulting multiplication and unpredictable timetable of elections become all the more unmanageable as the number of component units increases.

A federal regime presupposes a bicameral representation, since the component units are and must be represented in a separate body, be it senate or council. The cabinet can then be made dependent upon the confidence of either one house or the other, or both. If one house is chosen, as in Canada, it is necessarily given a predominant position which is apt to endanger the federal balance; if both are chosen, as in the Third French Republic, extreme instability results. As a consequence, it would seem that a federal regime is greatly benefited by, if it does not actually necessitate, a stable executive. The role of the opposition locally and nationally would suggest that different dates are desirable so as to avoid the submerging of local issues in national issues, and the carrying of local candidates on the wave of popularity of a national leader, as has often been observed in the United States. Certainly the operative range of the opposition would thereby be enhanced.

The executive's unifying role is usually greatly aided by some kind of arbitral or judicial body. Such a body can settle disputes concerning the meaning and interpretation of the treaty, charter, or constitution which the other federal authorities, especially the executive, are not able to compose. Again typically, the extent of the participation of the component communities in the selection and dismissal of such a body and its members is determined by the degree of federal diversity.

However constituted, such arbitral or judicial bodies are characteristi-

---

[12] This problem is, of course, not peculiar to federal regimes, but is ubiquitous in contemporary society. For the underlying theoretical and philosophical issues, cf. my *Constitutional Reason of State*, 1957. Compare also Chapter 10.

cally an instance of last resort, and whether or not they will forward the federalizing process, in either direction, will often depend upon circumstances of personal predilection or party politics, as the history of federal judiciaries clearly shows. The prevalence of arbitral, as compared with judicial, procedures will, roughly speaking, depend upon the state of the federalizing process: the more closely knit the federal system, the more formally judicial will these procedures become.[13]

One finds a judicial body for the settlement of disputes between the central and local authorities, as well as between the component units, in most federal systems. In the United States the Supreme Court, of course, is charged with this duty. Though on the whole favoring the federal government, it has not followed a consistent course. The same can be said of such federal judiciaries as those of Switzerland, Australia, and India.[14] The U. S. Supreme Court was nationally minded under Marshall, and several of his most famous decisions, like *McCulloch v. Maryland* and *Gibbons v. Ogden*, asserted doctrines that favored the central government. Later on, in the course of the slavery controversy the Court shifted toward a states' rights position which culminated in the ill-starred *Dred Scott* decision. After the Civil War, the Court turned back to its national orientation in some important economic fields, especially through the steady expansion of the interstate commerce clause, but it regrettably did not maintain the federal authorities in the civil rights field. In 1883, the Supreme Court held the Civil Rights Act to be beyond the power of Congress.[15] The Supreme Court has, admittedly and radically, reversed its position in recent years. Since it decided in *Baker v. Carr* in 1954 that segregation of American Negroes was a denial of their equal protection under the Constitution, and afterwards in 1963 disallowed the unlimited freedom of state legislatures to manipulate the apportionment of the electoral districts, the Court has resumed its vigorous defense of federal authority.

In Switzerland, where the court does not have the function to review the constitutionality of federal legislation, it is noteworthy that provisions about the administration of federal legislation by the cantons have not resulted in serious complications. This is probably owing to the fact that not a single canton is large in relation to the federation as a whole, that

[13] Felix Frankfurter and James M. Landis, *The Business of the Supreme Court—A Study in the Federal Judicial System*, 1928, fail to make this point explicit, though it is implicit in their account. Robert G. McCloskey, *The American Supreme Court*, 1960, Chapter 7 and others, describing the history of such courts have shown this general trend. Cf. Paul A. Freund, "Umpiring the Federal System," in Arthur W. MacMahon, ed., *Federalism: Mature and Emergent*, 1955.

[14] See for all this Arthur E. Sutherland, *Constitutionalism in America—Origin and Evolution of its Fundamental Ideas*, 1965, Chapters 13–15.

[15] See Burke Marshall, *Federalism and Civil Rights*, 1964, where Harlan is cited on page 84.

the cantons have not been sharply divided by partisan issues (neither Communism nor Fascism becoming sufficiently strong to be a threat), and that the central government has practiced marked moderation in employing force, relying rather upon persuasion and other kinds of pressure. The situation is rather different in the Federal Republic of Germany. This new and increasingly important Federal Constitutional Court has gradually become a champion on the *Länder*, "to enhance their position in the federal system." [16] The work of the court has been distinguished by the assumption of a degree of discretionary power in its decisions involving federal relationships, and more particularly its views on "federal loyalty" *Bundestreue*).[17] Whether one favors judicial "activism" or judicial "self-restraint," there can be little question that in effectively functioning federal systems, the umpiring of such a system by a constitutional court is of the essence.

Even though the federal division of powers is a mainstay of free constitutional government, it should not blind us to the fact that all governmental units share in the common task of accomplishing the "will of the people." Since the 1930s, the conviction has gained ground that "an emphasis on separateness or rivalry tends to forward the least desirable developments in American government today." [18] To put it thus may be to belittle the constitutional importance of divided powers; yet there is great merit in the view that "the sphere of government is increasing in its relation to life and there is a growth in both federal and state functions along a wide front."

In short, there has grown up a wide area of effective cooperation between the states and the federal government which is mutually advantageous and not necessarily destructive of the broader constitutional division of powers. The federal government stands in need of the more intimate contacts with local problems in such fields as social security, while on the other hand the local authorities in the poorer sections of the country may require the financial aid of the national government. The forms that such cooperation between the federal and state governments may take are many. Grants-in-aid, federal tax credits, cooperative use of personnel, as well as agreements and formal compacts, have been employed. In recent years there has been an increasing amount of dovetailing of legislation, examples of which include making federal laws contingent on state activities, sug-

[16] Gerhard Braunthal, "Federalism in Germany: The Broadcasting Controversy," 1962, 24; Donald R. Reich, "Court, Comity, and Federalism in Western Germany," 1963.

[17] Taylor Cole, "New Dimensions of West German Federalism," 1966 pp. 106 ff. Edward McWhinney, *Comparative Federalism—States' Rights and National Power*, 1962a, Chapter 3.

[18] Jane P. Clark, *The Rise of a New Federalism*, 1938.

gesting model statutes, and protecting through federal legislation one state against the unfair competition of another. There is, of course, forever present a fear that fiscal aids by the federal government may turn into means of compelling state action contrary to the preferences of the people's majority in the state. Even the fact that a state has sought federal aid under such conditions is no conclusive argument against the presence of compulsion. However, a measure of pressure such as we find in the fields of agriculture and education is probably desirable.

The trend toward concentration of economic power makes such cooperation well-nigh inescapable in the United States at the present time. Those fields of necessary regulation that the courts have withdrawn from the federal government's authority, in spite of the fact that the economic conditions make it inaccessible to the state authorities, may be handled by cooperative effort. The marketing of agricultural products is an outstanding example here. Although a number of objections are raised against the federal government's use of state personnel for the administration of federal legislation, the trend has been persistently forward in that direction.

The broadening scope of effective cooperation between state and federal agencies obscures the difference between a closely-knit federal setup and an effectively decentralized government such as that of England—so much so that years ago one could foresee the day when the character of a state is changed or modified into a kind of administrative unit to carry out federal plans and policies. The pressures and exigencies of a compact and highly industrialized national economy may eventually force the United States to abandon federalism. Although this would undoubtedly weaken the constitutional restraints in one important respect, it need not spell the end of constitutionalism. As the example of Canada (if not of England) shows, there are other methods available. A government—even a constitutional government—has to function effectively if it is to last.

The Second World War brought in its train a great many additional centralized activities. This trend has been reinforced by the plight of the cities in recent years. The draft, and price and rationing controls, as well as many of the directed production problems immediately growing out of the requirements of procurement for the armed services, all but swamped the American federal structure. This is perhaps nowhere as clearly visible as in the weight of the federal budget as compared with that of the states. Recently state and local governments have seen a rapid increase of their expenditures, due not only to price and wage increases but also to expanded functions.

It would be a mistake, however, to declare federalism in the United States dead; in some areas the states have recaptured some of their power through more vigorous insistence upon their participation in the federal administration. American federalism has, in other words, become cooperative federalism, and, in this, much more nearly resembles Swiss and German federalism than was formerly the case. This development in no wise conflicts with the advantages of divided power; the powers remain divided, even as they cooperate. The point has been well put in a Senate report on intergovernmental relations. " 'Cooperation' and 'coordination' are the key needs if we are to make federalism work under modern conditions . . . we are engaged in the task of assigning roles in the governmental processes.[19]

CONCLUSION The close link of constitutionalism with federalism has, I trust, become fully clear. Indeed, the rise of modern federalism coincides with that of constitutionalism, and the major theorists of constitutionalism have elaborated federalism. Neither of them is a creature of theoretical speculation, however. They both evolved slowly and in response to the problems of concrete situations for which they offered solution. At times, decentralization and, more particularly, local self-government, if constitutionally guaranteed and institutionalized, have served similar purposes, and the distinction between them and federal arrangements is at times difficult to draw. There is nothing in the distinction between federalism and decentralization that would imply an inherent superiority of one over the other, although such has been argued from time to time. Their advantages and disadvantages can only be compared in terms of the peculiar conditions of time and place. Federalism and/or constitutionally guaranteed local government are an integral part of modern constitutionalism.

A federal structure of government provides a territorial, as distinguished from a functional, separation of powers. Such a separation provides a rather effective restraint upon the abuse or misuse of governmental power. Such abuse may occur centrally or locally; many are the instances when the central authorities have uncovered local corruption, or when the local ones have helped defend the human rights of the citizens. Indeed, in numerous instances, the territorial division of power has proved more effective than the functional one. The party-sanctioned abuse of power occurs more often on the national than on the local plane, because parties succussfully circumvent the functional division. What federalism does is to mobilize firmly entrenched local powers in support of the constitution, offering them protection. Besides such negative and protective value, federalism and local government provide an opportunity for political experimentation in one or more of the local units.

Federal structures of government share with all formalized constitu-

---

[19] Senate Committee on Government Operations, *Intergovernmental Operations*, April 1, 1963. 88th Congress, Report 84.

tionalism the problems of adjusting a relatively rigid structure to the changing exigencies of a dynamic industrial society. Under modern industrial conditions, areas of friction and conflict are bound to develop where uncontrolled technological change radically alters the conditions under which government has to be conducted. If competencies are formally divided between the central and local authorities, as they are in most present-day federal systems, new governmental functions crystallize which can only be performed by one of them, or in close cooperation.

Without constitutional provisions new patterns of cooperation emerge, as has happened in the United States. Devices, such as grants-in-aid, may be expanded to take care of such situations.[20] Grodzins has coined the vivid simile that American federalism no longer resembles a layer-cake, but rather a marble-cake. That may be all very well as a temporary expedient, but the tie of federalism to constitutionalism demands that the marbling be explicitly defined and fixed in orderly rules and regulations.

In the United States as well as in Canada, schemes like tax-sharing are intended to solve some of the difficulties of federalism by redistributing the functions; delegating specific functions to the states and reinforcing such delegations by grants-in-aid have rapidly spread. Popular sentiment may be accurately reflected in statements such as Eisenhower's: "I am here because of my indestructible conviction that unless we preserve, in this country, the place of the State government, its traditional place—with the power, the authority, the responsibilities and the revenue necessary to discharge those responsibilities, then we are not going to have an America as we have known it; we will have some other form of government.[21] But the excluded alternative may yet be the actual future: an America different from what we have known. The very dynamics of federalism tend toward its own destruction: a centralized state in one case, a dissolution into fragments in the other.

[20] See for this Sundquist's *Making Federalism Work*, 1969; Chapter 1, p. 7, gives some striking statistics.

[21] Dwight D. Eisenhower, addressing the National Governors' Conference, 1953.

HUMAN RIGHTS
CONSTITUTIONAL
6

The American Constitution might have failed to be ratified if the more progressive politicians had not been assured that Congress would at once amend it by adding a bill of rights. It is curious that the lack of a bill of rights should have been the most effective argument against ratification. It was said that the new constitution was intended to deprive the people of their liberties. It is believed that the curious omission of such a bill was due to the argument that the constitutions of the states contained such guarantees by which the federal government would be restrained. A detailed list of limitations on the federal government seemed unnecessary because the national government could exercise only those powers enumerated in the Constitution.

It was a mistaken argument as subsequent history was to show,[1] but only an agreement to add such a bill of rights would overcome it. The argument demonstrates that human rights are not natural in the sense of being universal and self-enforcing, but have to be defined and guaranteed by a constitution. A modern Supreme Court Justice was to speak of these rights as provisions that "protect individual liberty." [2] In an earlier chapter (Chapter 3) the link between liberty and constitutionalism has been sketched, and it was there shown that these rights were meant to assure that each citizen

[1] See for this Arthur Sutherland, *Constitutionalism in America*, 1965, pp. 197 ff. The history of the rights under the American Constitution, as elsewhere, is a complex one; cf. my *The Impact of American Constitutionalism Abroad*, esp. Chapter 3. Z. Chafee, Jr., *How Human Rights Got Into the Constitution*, 1952, and his later *Human Rights in the Constitution*, 1956.

[2] Mr. Justice Hugo L. Black in his contribution to *The Great Rights*, ed. Edmond Cahn, 1963, p. 43. It was the formula of the French *Declaration* of 1789, but had been the core of British and American tradition in the seventeenth and eighteenth centuries. See for this tradition B. Mirkine-Guetzevich and M. Prelot, "Chrestomathie des Droits de l'Homme," *Politique, Revue Internationale des Doctrines et des Institutions*, 1960, Nrs. 10–13: 179 ff.

has a private sphere, by barring the government from acting in a particular area or from acting except under certain institutional procedures. This belief is at the very heart of constitutionalism in Britain and America.

In an early phase of development, the initial and primary rights proclaimed were those of conscience (religious belief) and property. In the course of the nineteenth century it gradually became clear that such rights were not something absolute and unchangeable.[3] As the rationalist beliefs of the preceding age acquired historical perspective, rights were recognized as constitutionally created and guaranteed. Comparisons of different "bills of rights" reinforced the conviction that such rights varied from time to time, and from place to place. Their adoption was seen as not merely an act of recognizing them, but of formulating and establishing them. Natural rights thus gradually were transformed into "civil liberties," the range of activities of the citizen. This transformation was, of course, closely linked to the forward march of democratization, and a marked shift in the assortment of such rights occurred, as the right to vote and participate in government and public policy formation became generally recognized and extended to the underprivileged and to women. The freedom of religion broadened into one of conviction; and academic freedom, the freedom to teach and to learn, was recognized even in countries like Germany and Austria-Hungary, where political participation was restricted. In the more advanced democratic countries, those rights that served the political function of better enabling the citizen to participate—freedom of the press, of assembly, and of association, often summed up in the general freedom of expression—moved into the foreground of attention, while the right of property was subjected to restrictions and limitations arising from the widely felt need for greater social control and for restraining the concentration of economic power.[4]

Civil liberties, vigorously advocated by progressive forces, often seemed to transcend to a great extent the individual and his personal interest. Civil liberties were the key issue in John Stuart Mill's *Liberty*, the classic statement of the libertarian doctrine in terms of social utility. Liberalism in its broadest connotation was the belief in these civil liberties and in the need for constitutionally protecting them.[5] This belief became associated with a great many more specific issues, political, economic and social, and it is

---

[3] Cf. my *Transcendent Justice*, 1964, Chapter 5. Cf. also the work cited in note 1, above. The U. S. Commission on Civil Rights has published a number of of valuable reports since 1959.

[4] A rather angry criticism of the trend away from the right of private property is found in Gottfried Dietze, *In Defense of Property*, 1963.

[5] John Stuart Mill, *On Liberty*, 1861, and Volume 5 of *Nomos*, entitled "Liberty" and devoted to an exploration of Mill's thought; note also that the definition given is of course not meant to be an exhaustive one; cf. my *Constitutional Government and Democracy*, 1968a), pp. 428 ff.

therefore possible to see these rights merely as rationalizations for a class interest, as Marx was inclined to do. Such an interpretation underlies the conception of rights in communist states. The notion of civil liberties was grounded in the conviction that freedom required social and political organization which would overcome both natural and man-made obstacles to the realization of individual freedom.[6]

Freedom of independence was being crowded by freedom of participation. Freedom of participation was actually the older.of the two. In the Greek cities it was this freedom rather than that of a personal sphere that had inspired such noble utterances as Pericles' Funeral Oration. The freedom of self-determination of "peoples" which the Draft Covenant of the Human Rights Convention of the United Nations proclaims in its article I (though it is not included in the Universal Declaration) is a modern version of this ancient freedom of classical Greece; the freedom of each man to live under a government belonging to the same national group as his own, as well as to participate therein.

One must not allow oneself to be misled by the collective form of this freedom to exclude it from the civil liberties. It is the civil liberty *par excellence* [7] and closely related to the freedom of participation and its collaterals. That this freedom may collide with, and at times even negate, other personal freedoms is undoubtedly true. But there are and always have been conflicts of principle between different liberties. Judicial interpretations of constitutional provisions concerning rights have had to weigh and balance conflicting claims of priority. Unless one were to construct a rigid hierarchy of these rights, or liberties, culminating in one highest and most important one, any broad recognition of rights will have to accept their pluralism.

At times it is argued that the personal rights of the inhabitants of former colonial territories were or are more firmly protected by the colonial power (contrast Hong Kong and Ghana, or Morocco before and after French domination). But the liberated people or at least their leaders will answer that the right of self-determination is a paramount right which precedes all personal rights.[8]

The civil liberties, including the right of self-determination, have, however, in the twentieth century been rivaled not only by the older personal rights, but also by the *freedoms* suggested in Roosevelt's proclamation and embodied in quite a few of the postwar constitutions as well as the

---

[6] Maurice Cranston, *Human Rights*, 1963; cf. also Leonard Krieger, "Stages in the History of Freedom," 1962, for perspective.

[7] Cranston, *Human Rights*, does not wish to admit this, and argues to the contrary. A similar position is adopted by Isaiah Berlin, *Two Concepts of Liberty*, 1958, pp. 44–45, who calls it a "hybrid form of freedom." Actually, it was already recognized during the French Revolution, following Rousseau.

[8] Cranston, *Human Rights*, pp. 66 ff.

United Nations' Universal Declaration of Human Rights.[9] These new freedoms are rights of an *economic* and *social* character which characteristically involve collective and more especially governmental effort. Among them are the right to security, to work,[10] to rest, to education, to an adequate standard of living, to participation in cultural life, and even to an international order ensuring these rights. Some of these rights which have come into prominence in the twentieth century actually appeared among other "natural" rights at an early date. Thus the French Declaration of May 29, 1973, declared in its article 22 that "education is the need of all and society owes it equally to all its members." [11] This declaration also clearly faced the need for government action; in its article 24 it asserted that the national sovereign (i.e., the people) must guarantee the enforcement of rights.

Only in the twentieth century, however, has the full significance of these social and economic rights become manifest. Such rights are obviously not protecting the individual against the government or other power-wielders, but call upon the public powers to see to it that such liberty as man possesses by himself is implemented by another set of freedoms which in contrast to those of independence and participation may be called freedoms of creation. They are rights that provide man with the freedom from fear and the freedom from want; that is to say, they liberate him from restrictions and inhibitions which hinder his full development as a human being. Although radically different from the older freedoms, they are nonetheless rightfully claimed for all men *qua* men. It is no longer permissible to brush these rights aside as less basic than the earlier ones or to question them because of the difficulty of effectuating them. All rights contain norms, and all norms fall short of their enforcement—if it were otherwise, why would norms be needed? The validity of a principle is not invalidated by its overextension.

Nor is it true to say that these rights are propounded by enemies of the established order, that the social rights, especially those associated with the freedom from want, are "communist" or "unamerican." Actually, Marx and Engels had little use for the tradition of natural or any other rights. The adoption and incorporation of them in the "constitutions" of Communist

---

[9] See my *The New Belief in the Common Man*, 1941, and Herbert Spiro, *Responsibility in Government: Theory and Practice*, 1969.

[10] The right to work is actually not new; it was explicitly urged even before the French Revolution by Turgot in the *Edit sur l'abolition des jurandes*, 1776. It appears in Robespierre's proposal of a restatement of the *Droits de l'homme et du Citoyen* of April 24, 1793. For these texts see P. Mirkine-Guetzevich and M. Prelot, "Chrestomathie des Droits de l'Homme," 1960. The classic *Declaration* is reprinted there on pp. 246–49. In this collection is also found the next *Declaration* of 1793.

[11] It was also urged by John Adams; see his *A Dissertation on Canon and Feudal Law* (1765), in *Works*, ed. Charles Francis Adams (Boston, 1850–1856), Vol. 3, pp. 456 f. But see Vol. 6, pp. 494 ff.

states is a part of the general function of such constitutions: to provide a facade of principles. All constitutions, of course, have this function to perform, and there is no gainsaying their role as myth. Still, the elaboration of these social rights in traditional constitutions was and is the result of protracted struggles by particular groups and minorities for equality and freedom. These rights, far from being "communist" or "unamerican," represent a response to a new and different situation of men frustrated by technological innovation and the like.

Recognizing these rights as true rights must not prevent their being seen as different from the older rights. In order to appreciate fully this difference between the three sets of rights, as evolved in the history of the last three hundred years, it is necessary first to determine what they have in common. If one takes these three rights, the right to one's religious conviction, the right to vote, and the right to work—three rights that illustrate the freedom of independence, the freedom of participation, and the freedom of creation, invention and innovation—one finds that, like the corresponding freedoms, these rights are all related to enabling a human being to become a rounded self, a fully developed person. Not to be allowed to believe what one does believe, not to participate in choosing one's ruler, not to be active in the sphere in which one could produce and create anew—every one of these deprivations is readily recognized as dehumanizing, as crippling the man so afflicted and preventing him from being a person in the full sense.

That it may be difficult to implement such rights, even after they are proclaimed, does not invalidate them, any more than the failure to claim a right makes it disappear. The rights that blacks now claim in the United States have been theirs for a long time, and their claims are based upon this very fact. Rights have an objective existence; they flow existentially from the recognized nature of man, as do the freedoms that correspond to them, for these freedoms are the manifestation of the power of human beings, of their capacity to put them to some account. Undoubtedly there exists, as far as capacity goes, a wide range of difference between individual human beings; but all men are capable of religious conviction, of voting, of working—to stay with our illustrations. The fact that each of the rights may be expressed as a capacity, as a power of man to achieve self-realization, is the hard core of all rights. Hence we may say that the most comprehensive right is the right to self-realization which has also been simply called the right to freedom.[12]

---

[12] Cf. the comment by C. W. Cassinelli in *Freedom, Control and Influence: An Analysis*, 1963, esp. Chapter 1, III. Kant, in his *Metaphysical Foundations of Morals* makes it clear that, dignity being the basis of man's right to freedom, from this right to fredeom follow all his other rights, political, legal and so on. See the selections in my *The Philosophy of Kant*, pp. 140 ff. Cf. also John Ladd's introduction, p. ix, to his translation of this work under the title *The Metaphysical Elements of Justice*. (Indianapolis: The Library of Liberal Arts, Bobbs-Merrill, 1965).

The most radical philosophical defense of the premise of such a position is found in Baruch Spinoza's *Theological-Political Treatise:* "The natural right of the individual man is thus determined, not by sound reason, but by desire and power." [13] Such an identification of right and power sounds strange in the perspective of many human rights enthusiasts who claim rights on behalf of underprivileged groups and individuals. Yet, it could be persuasively argued that the dramatic change in the position of the American Negro highlighted by the Supreme Court decision referred to below was the result of the changing power position of the blacks. Their by-now-familiar rhetoric about black power reinforces such an argument.

Napoleon Bonaparte, though a child of the French Revolution, once proclaimed that the destiny of man was obedience: "he deserves nothing better, and he has no rights." Similar views have been entertained by authoritarians in many places. Alexander Hamilton was opposed to the inclusion of a bill of rights in the American Constitution, and effectively thwarted it, until forced to concede the point by popular pressure. Otto von Bismarck, Germany's Iron Chancellor and founder of the Empire, kept a bill of rights out of the Imperial constitution. Marx and Engels had no use for bills of rights; they thought that these were bourgeois prejudices, calculated to dupe the masses about the exploitative character of the bourgeois state.

Twentieth-century totalitarians have been inclined to adapt such a view to their own purposes. The constitutions of the Soviet Union and other Communist regimes have proclaimed such rights. But they made no effort to provide enforcement machinery, so that they remained facades behind which the autocratic rule by party and dictator could try to hide.[14] These developments have brought to light a basic difference of rights in their relation to self. Rights appear to be either self-preserving, self-asserting, or self-developing. Looked at in the perspective of the political order of the community, such rights are either rights apart from this political order of the community, rights directed toward the political order, or rights depending upon the political order (Rights A, B, and C). These classes of rights are not sharply delimited and cannot be precisely separated from each other. Consider, e.g., the right of property which has undergone such a remarkable evolution in the course of the last 150 years. It may be seen as either of the three rights: to be protected from government interference (no taxation without representation—Right A); to serve as the basis of voting (Right B); or for small business to be protected against unfair competition by big business (Right C). It is evident that the right to one's property is a basic

---

[13] Baruch Spinoza, *Theologico-Political Treatise*, Ch. 16, in Bohn's edition (London: George Bell & Sons, 1900), Vol. 1, p. 201.

[14] Merle Fainsod, *How Russia is Ruled*, rev. ed., 1963, pp. 375 ff. Cf. my (with Z. Brzezinski) *Totalitarian Dictatorship and Autocracy*, rev. ed., 1965, Ch. 10.

right, but property may involve any one of the three kinds of rights. As a consequence, it is even in some Communist political orders beginning to be recognized as a right.

Another reflection will serve to reinforce the insight into this interconnectedness of the three kinds of rights. A right may be legally recognized and deeply felt by the person deprived of it; yet the deprivation may be caused by a nongovernmental power-holder and -wielder. In this case, what appears at first to be a right apart from the political order may turn out to be a right depending upon the political order. This is typically the situation of underprivileged minorities, such as blacks in the United States. Still another facet of this interconnectedness may be seen in the early recognition of the right to education, at a time when generally prevalent thought dwelt on natural rights of independence. Thus we find John Adams writing that "liberty cannot be preserved without a general knowledge among the people, who have a right, from the frame of their nature, to knowledge." This right to education, now generally included among the economic and social rights, and surely a right depending upon the political order, was even then by this conservative New Englander described as an "inherent and essential right," a right, that is, which was established "even before parliament existed." [15]

Often the rank order of and the distinction between the different rights is relative to the status of the particular person in the social order. Thus, the inherent right to an education is for a wealthy person a right *apart from* the political order, whereas for the poor one it is a right *depending upon* the political order. Thus a right to education may be recognized and yet not be effective in a community where much of the best education is offered in universities with very high tuition charges, unless scholarship funds are made readily available without discrimination for underprivileged persons. Much of the present struggle over desegregated educational opportunity for blacks is similarly related to the neighborhoods in which blacks live and where facilities are inferior to standards maintained elsewhere.

Thus the problem of Negro education is, first of all, one of equal facilities. Although rapid progress has been achieved toward the "closing of the gap," a great deal remains to be done, and it is a problem by no means restricted to the South. The issue transcends, however, that of facilities. To recall, the Supreme Court unanimously held "separate educational facilities are inherently unequal," because "to separate them [black children] from others of similar age and qualification solely because of their race generates a feeling of inferiority as to their hearts and minds in a way unlikely ever to be overcome." [16] Not only in providing facilities but in securing equal

[15] Cf. Page Smith, *John Adams*, 1962, Vol. 1, p. 79.

[16] *Brown v. Board of Education of Topeka*, 347 U.S. 483 (1954), overruling the decision of *Plessy v. Ferguson* (1896), which had established the principle of

access to all schools, the government may have exacting responsibilities in enforcing the rights of the weaker against the stronger.

The current controversy over busing illustrates this. The whites who object to the busing of children between school districts are bringing their residual power (as voters) to bear upon a situation in which the right of one group involves the deprivation of right of another. There is rarely a clear and straight answer in such situations where different rights clash, and hence courts cannot provide an adequate answer. They involve one of the most difficult paradoxes of the human rights problem, namely whether there exists or ought to exist a rank list establishing priorities (see below).

Such an active role of the government (state) is also recognized as needed in the economic sphere. The neo-liberals in Europe, like the progressives in the United States, have been stressing the importance of firm government action to cope with the threats to freedom and man's rights resulting from monopoly power. Beyond that, the government must be able to assert its authority when facing the interest groups that press upon it from all sides. Yet in granting the government the position of a powerful arbiter mediating the conflicts of interest, neo-liberals are not prepared to abandon their basically critical attitude toward it. Order and rule are needed to maintain freedom, but vigorous restraints are needed to contain the rulers within the bounds of a constitutional order which protects human rights. Like Hegel and John Stuart Mill, they would stress the primacy of the political, and hold that *order* is a prime requisite for freedom and the maintenance of human rights.[17]

Neo-liberalism, by stressing the role of the government in the maintenance of freedom, contributes its share to an understanding of the fact that all rights are political in the sense of depending upon the political order for their maintenance and enforcement. They are political in the further sense of depending upon the values and beliefs of the political community that the order serves. Many of the newer rights are evidently the corollary of fairly recent developments; thus the right to work was only recognized generally when industrialization created large-scale unemployment. Still, it would be a mistake to make this the ground for asserting that this right only came into being at that point. Rather, the assertion of the right is

---

equal but separate education. The situation existing under that principle is admirably analyzed and put into context by Gunnar Myrdal, with Richard Sterner and Arnold Rose, *An American Dilemma*, 1944, Chapter 41. Cf. also the discussion in *The Report of the United States Commission on Civil Rights*, 1959, and the helpful abridgment entitled *With Liberty and Justice for All*, 1959, esp. Part 3, pp. 101–37. The rapid progress which is being made in equalizing facilities can be gleaned from SERS, *Southern Schools: Progress and Problems*, 1959, especially the valuable statistical material; cf. also the special issue of the *Harvard Educational Review*, Summer 1960, entitled "Negro Education in the United States."

[17] See my article, "The Political Thought of Neoliberalism," 1955. Cf. Hegel, *The Philosophy of Law and Right*, in my *The Philosophy of Hegel*, 1953, pp. 257 ff.

rooted in the belief that it is part of man's nature to work and that therefore any situation that deprives him of fulfilling this natural propensity ought to be corrected.[18]

This reflection reinforces the important insight already mentioned, that rights are characteristically normative in the sense that they reflect a tension between what is and what ought to be. From this vantage point, it can be seen that a right is related to an aspect of human nature that is being inhibited or thwarted. Such tension may be felt by those who are the victims of such torts or it may not. But as already mentioned, whether they are or not, is not determinative. Established rights which have become conventional are often shrouded in forgetfulness until some dramatic issue projects them into the full glare of publicity. A recent case will illustrate the point. The Massachusetts Supreme Judicial Court held illegal and unconstitutional a practice connected with special taxes on liquor and consisting in the state police stopping cars and searching them for various items of merchandise. This practice, justified in the name of law enforcement, was a flagrant violation of the right of privacy, more especially the right to be protected against searches and seizures without judicial warrant. The court in its opinion added that a warrant must be specific, name the person, and specify the grounds of reasonable suspicion in the particular case. For many people, it was news and good news that they possessed this right.[19]

The failure of men everywhere to appreciate the rights that they possess, or indeed to know about them, or to realize what means are available for vindicating them, creates great obstacles to their enforcement, for unless complaint is made and insisted upon, law enforcement authorities often cannot act. It has been argued, as to conditions in the United States, that "individuals have less and less recourse to any corrective remedy against those who hold positions of power." [20] Such a view probably exaggerates the sound point that serious injustice may develop and continue to prevail because of the ignorance and indifference of the underprivileged.

A poll in Puerto Rico disclosed that only a small percentage of the people knew what were their rights; similar conditions have been found to exist in India, Germany, and elsewhere.[21] Likewise, many Americans, especially black Americans, do not appreciate the rights that they possess and could rightfully claim. For generations since the Civil War blacks in many

---

[18] See footnote 10 above.

[19] *Commonwealth v. Michael C. McCleary*, Nov. 29, 1962.

[20] Justice William O. Douglas in *The Great Right*, ed. Cahn, 1963, p. 149.

[21] See Comite del Gobernador para el Estudio de los Derechos Civiles en Puerto Rico, *Informe al Honorable Governador del Estado Libro Asociado de Puerto Rico*, 1959. The lack of knowledge in the United States is affirmed by Douglas in the paper cited, p. 155, footnote 20 above.

states have, for example, been prevented from exercising their right to vote. Hostile white authorities interfered with their registering. Since in a democratic society political representatives are in the habit of acting in response to their constituency, nonregistration of Negroes proved the most effective method of silencing them. The ruthless and violent ways in which this deprivation was accomplished have been described many times; [22] the silent deprivation through ignorance and desuetude went more commonly unnoticed. By these means, the constitutional amendment forbidding all discrimination was blandly nullified.[23] The power resources of those blacks who wished to insist upon their rights were not sufficiently developed to secure their enforcement. Recently, their organizations have been gaining sufficient strength to assert their right to vote as well as other rights. As a result, the United States government now finds itself obliged to enforce rights which it might, theoretically, have enforced long ago.

The consequences of ignorance and intimidation are even more serious where the established government is violating or participating in the violation of human rights. Totalitarian governments apart, in many countries where rights, liberties, and freedoms have only recently become constitutionally recognized, they have remained largely paper declarations. It might be invidious to mention particular instances, but not one of the countries that have adopted constitutions since the Second World War has a satisfactory record of enforcement of its constitutional bill of rights. Rare are the instances where the public has been ready to take a vigorous stand. The *Spiegel* affair in the German Federal Republic was significant primarily on this account.[24]

A special aspect of this range of problems is the question of "states' rights" under federal systems. In these systems, the question of human rights, whether of broad or limited scope, is often argued in terms of a juxtaposition to states' rights. Especially in the United States, but also in relation to the United Nations' *Declaration*, it is argued that the rights of

[22] This was perhaps never more vividly and movingly done than by Howard Fast in his historical novel, *Freedom Road*, 1969. Cf. also Paul H. Buck, *Road to Reunion*, 1937, pp. 67 and 276 ff.

[23] For a descriptive account, see V. O. Key, Jr., *Southern Politics*, 1949, Chapter 26. Amendment XIV, in the second sentence states: "No state shall make or enforce any law which shall abridge the privileges and immunities of citizens of the United States; . . ." Yet in spite of the imperative form of the language, such privileges and immunities (rights) have been abridged continually, and the efforts to secure a remedy through the courts and legislatures have been successful only to a very limited extent. The inherent difficulties have been analyzed rather persuasively by Jack W. Peltason, *Fifty-eight Lonely Men*, 1961.

[24] For the *Spiegel* affair, see David Schoenbaum, *Ein Abgrund von Landesverrat—Die Affaire um den Spiegel*, 1968; the briefer original American version was entitled *The Spiegel Affair*, 1968.

individual men must yield to the rights of collectivities. There seems to be good ground for such an assertion, insofar as history has shown and daily experience confirms considerable variations in what are believed to be basic rights. Rights, as we have seen, are closely linked to the conception of man in particular communities, and it is for each political community to determine them in range and rank. But this argument is rather superficial; it fails to take into account the fact that any particular local manifestation of such rights is embedded in the broader and more basic conception of these rights as belonging to human beings as such. Thus the United Nations *Declaration* aspires to state what is now universally recognized as part of the rights of all men, and the same may be said of the European Declaration for all Europeans. The argument applies *a priori* to all Americans who together constitute one political community. Local variations may be admissible within the broad context of such rights as flow from the freedom of expression, but they may not take the form of a denial of the right. In other words, states' rights ought not to be pleaded against human rights within a federal system, except where the constitution explicitly permits local diversity. In case of doubt, the presumption must be in favor of the human right; in the United States man is considered more important than the state.

But there are, of course, limitations to any right, especially that of possible hurt to another. As the United Nations *Declaration* puts it: "In the exercise of his rights and freedoms, everyone shall be subject only to such limitations as are determined by law solely for the purpose of securing due recognition and respect for the rights and freedoms of others. . . ." [25] Had the *Declaration* left it at that, there could have been little objection. Freedom has traditionally been seen as limited by regard for the rights of others.[26] But actually, the *Declaration* adds another limitation which might and surely could nullify all effective rights. It goes on to say that the exercise of such rights is limited by "the purpose of meeting the just requirements of morality, public order and the general welfare in a democratic society." In view of the different conceptions of democracy, ranging from Swiss constitutional democracy to the totalitarian system of Mao's China, it is evident that such terms as public order and general welfare, not to mention morality, are so vague in their implications as to enable the rulers to justify any limitation they see fit to impose. Indeed, such vague limitations are apt to render rights nugatory. Bills of rights, under such regimes

[25] United Nations *Declaration*, Art. 29.

[26] Kant's formula is perhaps the most widely known, but is also found in Locke and many others in similar forms; perhaps Kant's owes its fame to the explicitly imperative form: "Act so that . . . ," *Die Metaphysik der Sitten* (Immanuel Kant's *Werke*, ed. E. Cassirer, Volume 7, Pt. I, p. 17.) Cf. also the comprehensive review by Mortimer Adler, *The Idea of Freedom*, Vol. 1, 1958.

as the popular democracies, become purely declaratory and unenforceable; they constitute essentially declarations of the principles and goals which the regime wishes the world at large to believe them to be dedicated to.[27]

In this perspective it becomes clear why rights depend for their effectualization upon the marshalling of appropriate power. It is precisely such marshalling of power that, for example, the organization of labor and of deprived racial minorities seeks to accomplish. In his by now famous *Letter from a Birmingham Jail*, the Rev. Martin Luther King, Jr. pointed out: "We have not made a single gain in civil rights without determined legal and nonviolent pressure. . . . We know through painful experience that freedom is never voluntarily given by the oppressor; it must be demanded by the oppressed." [28]

Such demands are futile and ineffectual, unless they are organized demands; the power of the many lies in the capacity to organize. Although significant remedial measures may also be possible as a result of invoking the intervention of higher powers, these possibilities are limited even in the United States. When the federal government is being mobilized against state governments which fail to implement federally guaranteed rights, it is not always sufficiently powerful to be able to cope with the situation. In Europe, a court and commission have commenced to enforce human rights which particular governments may be inclined to disregard; it is of course, only a beginning.[29]

It had been the expectation of some that the United Nations' *Universal Declaration* would similarly by covenant be given effective enforcement machinery, but such hopes have been disappointed up to the present time.[30] In most cases, therefore, the fuller implementation of recognized rights depends upon the power individuals can marshal through organization, whether for the display of coercive power as in strikes, for the purpose of effective pleading before courts, for exerting pressure for needed legislation, or for securing remedial action in the administrative field. Hence,

---

[27] Karl Löwenstein, *Verfassungslehre*, 1959, pp. 153 ff., has developed the notion of a semantic constitution; in analogy one could speak of "semantic" human rights. Cf. Giovanni Sartori, "Constitutionalism: A Preliminary Discussion," 1962a, argues for the term "façade" constitution.

[28] The letter of Rev. Martin Luther King, Jr. has been reprinted in various journals; I have used the reprint in *The New Leader*, July 1963. There is a remarkable similarity between this letter and some of the arguments in James Baldwin's *Nobody Knows My Name*, 1961, esp. Part 1, sections 3-6.

[29] D. P. Myers, "The European Commission on Human Rights," 1956; A. H. Robertson, "The European Court of Human Rights," 1959. More recent assessments include "European Law—Does It Exist?", 1966, and G. Treves, ed., *Diritto delle Communita Europee e Diritto degli Stati Membri*, 1969.

[30] A. H. Holcombe, *Human Rights in the Modern World*, 1948; H. Lauterpacht, *International Law and Human Rights*, 1951.

any political order that prevents individuals from organizing themselves for the defense of their rights *as they see them* is unlikely to provide adequate scope for the maintenance of such rights. The near impossibility of autonomously organizing groups of citizens in totalitarian orders testifies to the weakness of human rights in such states.[31]

The problem of the enforcing of rights under a constitution is intimately bound up with the problem of the rank order of rights in a particular political order. It is this priority of rights that demonstrates the dependence of all rights upon law and more typically upon constitutional law. They constitute, in their range and sophistication, major inventions of the kind that human ingenuity and creativity have contributed to the evolution of the political order. Nor is the end in sight by any means.

The older constitutional systems are particularly in need of revision and radical innovation. Advance is needed, and it is more likely to be achieved at the polls or constitutional conventions than in courts; it is part of the *political* process to achieve them. The American Bill of Rights, so called, is no longer adequate. Not only has there been a certain attenuation of older rights which need to be reaffirmed and strengthened,[32] but some of the new rights urgently require constitutional sanction. Thus the right to an adequate education, guaranteed in a number of the newer constitutions as well as the United Nations' *Declaration,* ought to be positively affirmed in the United States Constitution. It would provide the courts with the necessary ground for coping with certain grave abuses, such as the withholding of education from broad classes of citizens because of local dissatisfaction with the standards (desegregation) demanded under the Constitution. The right to be educated is possibly an even more important right than the right to be admitted to a particular school. Similarly, the right to work, while promoted by much federal legislation, may be denied by state and local authorities, when only their jurisdiction is involved.

The problem presents itself in particularly poignant form in connection with the right to vote. The denial of that right through the handling of registration (mentioned above) appears to be an abuse, because the general right of participation in politics, of which the right to vote is an important part, is today universally acknowledged to be basic to a free community; how that right is being exercised, whether, for example, through proportional or majoritarian representation, whether by people

---

[31] C. J. Friedrich and Z. K. Brzezinski, *Totalitarian Dictatorship and Autocracy,* rev. ed., 1967, Chapter 20 and the literature there cited. A number of writers, notably H. Gordon Skilling, have recently insisted upon pluralistic group conflict in the Soviet Union and other Communist states; cf. H. Gordon Skilling and Franklin Griffiths, eds., *Interest Groups in Soviet Politics,* 1970.

[32] Mr. Justice Douglas in Cahn, *The Great Right,* pp. 146 ff. The legislation on civil rights before Congress seeks to accomplish just that.

over 21 or over 18, and such like questions, may, on the other hand, well be left to local determination. Anyone comparing the traditional bill of rights derived from the eighteenth and nineteenth centuries, with the modern bills of rights, making full allowance for social rights, will appreciate the need for radical revision.

But even when every effort is being made to reshape the constitutionally guaranteed rights in accordance with a wider and more adequate conception of human freedom, the problem remains of how to combine the several rights, liberties, and freedoms into a balanced and harmonious whole. This problem cannot be solved by arranging these rights, liberties, and freedoms into a rank list of simple priorities. The problem is not one-dimensional and static, but multi-dimensional and dynamic. It can only be solved in approximation and through constitutional procedures for its solution in response to specific situations and particular circumstances.

The problem of the rank order of various rights has, in American law as well as in other legal orders, been partially answered in terms of the sequence in which such rights occur. Thus, the First Amendment has very generally been claimed to be foremost and to contain those rights that are preeminent.[33] This assertion must be considered dubious, in spite of the prevailing view, if for no other reason than because a number of important rights are scattered throughout the original Constitution, including the crucial one of *habeas corpus*. In any case, giving the First Amendment preeminence does not eliminate the problem of rank order, because the First Amendment itself contains a number of rights that may readily conflict with each other. For example, regulatory provisions protecting the individual's freedom of expression (speech) over the air may interfere with the private property rights of the owner of the broadcasting facilities. Not only property rights, but other rights, may be in conflict. Freedom of the press clashes with the right of privacy, as well as the right to a fair trial and other rights.

Many other examples could be adduced, especially as between the older rights which are self-preserving and the newer rights which are self-developing. The reasons are not far to seek; for the former favor the well-to-do, indeed all the *beati possidentes*, while the latter favor the poor. It is in the very nature of such rights that they cannot be ranked in a fixed order, because the more or less in each case must be taken into account. A small infringement of a right A and a great loss in a right C, for example, may call for one decision, whereas the reverse may call for the opposite decision. "Situation sense" on the part of judges, legislators, and

---

[33] *Everson v. Board of Education*, 330 U.S. 1 (1947); cf. also the interesting discussion of the problem of priority in particular reference to economic due process in Robert G. McCloskey, "Economic Due Process and the Supreme Court: An Exhumation and Reburial," 1962.

administrators will be required at all times; carefully elaborated procedures which make the cautious weighing of alternatives possible are the only way to secure maximum realization of all the different rights of protection.

By the way, judges are not always the most vigorous guardians of human rights, though some judges at some times have rendered outstanding service.[34] Nor can any other authorities be relied upon for such protection, unless an alert public is constantly on the watch and ready, individually and collectively, to insist upon the enforcement of the rights it recognizes as expressing the community's values, interests, and beliefs. The old saying that eternal vigilance is the price of freedom has lost none of its relevance, nor has the evangelical assertion that "the truth will make you free." Such truth is not given, settled and final, but is set as a task.[35] In the last analysis, only the common man himself can be the guardian of his rights, the rights common to all men. What the intellectual needs to remember, and often does not, is that he too is a common man, that is to say, a communal man (as contrasted with the mass man) when he steps into the marketplace and participates in the affairs of the community.

In the ranking of rights, one cannot hope to arrive at a definitive settlement even individually and for oneself. For a political community of any size it is out of the question that more be agreed upon than what rights to include in a general bill and a procedure for settling the issues as they arise, legislatively, judicially, administratively.

The question of rank order resembles in some respects the problem of how to balance rights against other considerations, such as those of security. As our preceding discussion has shown, these issues often are in fact conflicts over which right to give priority. Notably, in the matter of security the right of protection, which has often been taken to be the most basic right, is involved. It is, therefore, not very useful to argue that "there *are* 'absolutes' in our Bill of Rights, and that they were put there on purpose . . ."[36] for the question really is not whether the rights are absolute or relative to the public interest (though admittedly the argument is often cast in these terms). The question is, rather, whether any among the rights are to be preferred to others, and if so, which ones. What the answer can be we have just shown.

At this point, the grave issues of the survival of a constitutional order—in classical terms the problem of constitutional reason of state— must be faced. They will occupy the next chapter. Here it remains to re-

---

[34] Benjamin N. Cardozo, *The Nature of the Judicial Process,* 1921; the literature on this subject is, of course, very large.

[35] Cf. my *The New Belief in the Common Man,* 1941, in which the destructive pessimism of Erich Fromm's *Escape from Freedom,* 1941, is rejected.

[36] Mr. Justice Black in Cahn, *The Great Right,* esp. pp. 57 ff.

mark further on the issues of academic freedom and of the freedom of the press as they arise with regard to the mass media operated by large commercial corporations. It is customary for these groups to claim the protection of freedom of the press as a basic human right guaranteed by the constitution. Now it is certainly true that the founders, notably Thomas Jefferson, believed in a free press. At times, it was even asserted by Jefferson that such a press was more important than the government—a rather dubious assertion! [37] It may, however, be doubted that Jefferson would be prepared to extend these judgments to the corporate enterprises of the modern mass media. In discussions over the freedom of the press, it is also often forgotten that in the eighteenth century the word "press" referred to the printing presses and not to the collective mass media that use printing for their communications. Its freedom referred to the right of every citizen to set up a little printing press and issue his own pamphlets—an activity that had been unlawful in Britain and subject to severe penalties! The Hearsts, Beaverbrooks, and Springers cannot be duplicated by the citizen, and in that perspective the freedom of the press has been destroyed or at any rate severely limited by the development of large corporate enterprises.

The advent of radio broadcasting produced a new dimension of this problem; licensing was necessitated by the technical limitations of air channels, and "the public interest" safeguarded by a regulatory commission that administers such regulations.[38] Some of such regulations are intended to protect the freedom of speech, but in spite of them the average citizen has no freedom to speak over the broadcasting channels, whether privately owned, as in the United States, or public, as in Great Britain and the European continent; only minimal chances are provided for such freedom of speech. Against all such regulations, the owners are in the habit of pleading the freedom of the press which they by analogy claim for radio broadcasting—providing a typical case of the conflict of rights discussed above.

Lately the extravagant claims on behalf of the press have been broadened by the invention of a new right, the right of the people to be informed (about governmental secrets). There is, of course, no provision in constitutions of any such right which is said to be implied in the right to vote. It is said that the right to vote is meaningless, if the voter is not adequately informed. It is a rationalist argument which will be more fully discussed in the next chapter.

The right to be informed is related to the right of a free man to be

---

[37] Letter, Jan. 10, 1787 to Col. Edward Carrington. "Were it left to me to decide whether we should have a government without newspapers, or newspapers without a government, I should not hesitate a moment to prefer the latter."

[38] See Chapter 23 of my *Constitutional Government and Democracy*, 1968a, for further detail, and the literature cited there.

educated. Such education itself raises very difficult questions: what is to be the content and who is to determine the content of what is taught—the community and its representatives (ministries of education, school boards, etc.), the teachers, the parents, or the children? Every one of these alternatives has found convinced advocates, and it has usually been claimed by each contestant that his answer is more democratic than others.[39] The alternative according to which teachers are the right persons to determine the content of education has in the past been especially insisted upon in connection with higher education on the university level. In this field, the claim has been expressed in terms of academic freedom.

This particular freedom is constitutionally safeguarded in the German Constitution of the Federal Republic in the lapidary statement: "Art and learning, research and teaching are free." Similar assertions are found in most of the state constitutions of the Federal Republic.[40] It is not constitutionally guaranteed in English-speaking countries,[41] but is widely claimed. Its meaning is therefore quite controversial; an authoritative encyclopedia defines it, in its "primary sense," as follows: it is "the freedom claimed by a college or university professor to write or speak the truth as he sees it, without fear of dismissal." [42] Such a definition is defective in that it does not limit this right to speak the truth to academic halls which is essential for its justification.

Outside academic institutions, the teacher is entitled only to that freedom of speech that all other citizens possess. He is not a specially

[39] See "Independence of Thought and Propaganda" and "The Future Citizen," both in my The New Image of the Common Man, 2nd ed., 1950, Chapters 3 and 9. The student rebels of recent years have particularly stressed the academic freedom of students and their right to co-determine what is being taught. Cf. Bryan Wilson, The Youth Culture and the Universities, 1970; Helmut Kuhn, Jugend im Aufbruch, 1970; Wilhelm Hennis, Die deutsche Unruhe—Studien zur Hochschulpolitik, 1969, esp. pp. 79 ff. Cf. also the document "Studenten und die neue Universitaet," 1962.

[40] Gerhard Leibholz and H. J. Rink, Grundgesetz—Ein Kommentar, 1944, pp. 121 ff. The text of the constitution reads in the third paragraph of article V: (III) "Kunst und Wissenschaft, Forschung und Lehre sind frei. Die Freiheit der Lehre entbindet nicht von der Treue zur Verfassung." The second, limiting sentence implies a certain ideological commitment which is at times forgotten by those who argue in terms of academic freedom.

[41] A significant, but very limited exception is a provision in the constitution of the Commonwealth of Massachusetts. See for this George K. Gardner, "The Constitutional Questions Raised by the Flag Salute and Teachers' Oath Acts in Massachusetts," 1936.

[42] "Academic Freedom" by Glenn R. Morrow, in International Encyclopedia of the Social Sciences, Vol. 1, 1968. Richard Hofstadter and Walter P. Metzger, The Development of Academic Freedom in the United States, 1955; Russell Kirk, Academic Freedom—An Essay in Definition, 1955; Robert M. McIver, Academic Freedom in Our Time, 1955. The American Association of University Professors has published various articles in its Bulletin from time to time.

privileged person, but one with a particular function to perform for which the right to speak the truth is necessary. The other defect of the definition is that it limits academic freedom to the teachers; it is also the right or the freedom to learn the truth (and is so stated in German constitutions), and hence extends to students. Unfortunately, academic freedom has been unduly extended (and thereby weakened) to protect academic personnel when speaking or publishing in public; this would made academic people privileged citizens which is incompatible with democratic constitutionalism. It is not a valid objection, of course, to intellectual elitism and its aristocratic implications—a view to which many academics incline, often unconsciously.[43]

Basic human rights, a key aspect of modern constitutionalism, though absent in classical antiquity, are variable in content and by no means either natural or unchangeable. Their source is not some kind of natural law which may, however, provide a rationalization or legitimation. Their source is the popular will, as expressed in a constitution. They are not natural, but political; they are intended to be inviolable and unalienable, except by formal constitutional amendment. They express the basic values cherished in a particular political community; many of them are shared by most of mankind, as expressed in the *Universal Declaration of Human Rights,* adopted by the United Nations. No legal document that lacks specified human rights and provisions for their enforcement can be said to be a genuine constitution in the tradition of Western constitutionalism.

---

[43] Professors in Germany have banded together and formed a *Bund—Freiheit der Wissenschaft,* to defend traditional academic (professorial) freedom against its assailants among students and politicians.

CONSTITUTIONAL CRISIS

7

Human rights create an issue of perplexing complexity when they are being claimed by enemies of the constitutional order. They may be used to destroy the order upon which they rest. Freedom of religion (conviction) may be abused to preach subversion, and so may freedom of speech be claimed for revolutionary doctrines, freedom of the press for circulating material destructive of the belief system upon which the constitution rests, and so forth, and so on. Situations may arise, however, where the survival of the constitution itself requires measures which, to a greater or lesser degree, are incompatible with the maintenance of human rights. If the existing constitutional order is to be preserved under these circumstances, the constitutional framework must either explicitly anticipate the need for emergency action, or else be given enough inherent flexibility to enable the government to deal with emergencies by means of extraordinary devices. The question, in either case, is to provide for the temporary relaxation of constitutional restraints without permanently impairing the norms of constitutional government. This is the problem of "emergency powers," on the solution of which the maintenance of constitutional order to a large extent depends.

The crises which have required the exercise of emergency powers are of five main types. Three of these are war, economic depression, and secession. They represent a deliberate refusal on the part of certain members of a constitutional society to accept the legitimate procedures of that society as binding upon their own present or future action. The disaffected members are striving to change the constitutional order. Insurrection and subversion are, by definition, attempts to act in violation of constitutional procedures. Unwillingness to abide by the established processes of constitutional government gives rise to very special problems within any constitutional order, and this must be faced by the philosophy of constitutionalism, though often gainsaid.

The problem of survival is common to all kinds of government. The moral issues involved arise wherever a religion makes absolute claims upon its believers. Thus the problem of reason of state, so-called, arose. Since religious responsibility means that a man has to account for his actions in terms of transcendant ethical norms, it involves particular pitfalls for the ruler and official who seeks to be guided by it. Situations are bound to occur in which such norms conflict with the exigencies of the conduct of government. The proverbial saying about ambassadors that they are men sent abroad to lie for the good of their country epitomizes this difficulty. The ruler or official who obeys the moral law may lose out to his rival.

To have observed and described such situations with corrosive frankness was one of Machiavelli's achievements. He challenged much "conventional wisdom" about government. His own resolution of the difficulty was to make the state the highest value and the source of all human virtue. He could then blandly claim that no real conflict existed, because to build and maintain a state was man's highest achievement, his greatest work of art. Thus his frankly "ancient wisdom," derived he thought from Greek and Roman historians, was of course unacceptable to most of his Christian contemporaries. They had to try to reconcile the requirements of statecraft with Christian morals. The result was the doctrine of reason of state.[1] It is actually merely a specific form of the kind of rationality that places organization requirements (an operational code) above a moral code.

Constitutional reason of state in its subtler, modern form raises the question: how can one, how must one, deal with declared enemies of the constitutional order, *any* constitutional order, when such men are as citizens entitled to the protection of that constitution? Are they entitled to enjoy the fundamental rights and civil liberties? The answers range all the way from completely denying any such rights of "subversive elements" to fully vindicating them for "enemies of the constitution." Security and survival of the state, or more especially of the good state, of the constitutional, civilized political order, has challenged the ingenuity of the best constitutionalists, from Locke to Hegel and into our own time. But no entirely satisfactory answer has been found. Constitutional reason of state is, in the last analysis, a matter of ever more effectively ordering a constitutional community's internal and external relations. If constitutionalism is based upon the belief

---

[1] See my *Constitutional Reason of State: The Survival of the Constitutional Order,* 1957, and the literature cited there, more specifically Friedrich Meinecke, *Die Idee der Staatsraison in der neueren Geschichte,* 1924, of which an English translation by D. Scott appeared in 1965 under the title *Machiavellism: The Doctrine of Raison d'Etat and its Place in Modern History.* The basic source is Giovanni Botero, *Della Ragion di Stato,* 1589. An English translation was prepared by P. J. and D. P. Waley, 1956.

that the most fundamental of all the rights is the right of a man to his conviction, his faith, the hard core of man's dignity, then its very survival is at stake in its protection. To make his innermost self secure is more vital to the security and survival of a constitutional order than any secret. It defines the boundary beyond which no expedient measures can be permitted to go in safeguarding the system's survival.[2]

Christopher Marlowe, in his play *The Jew of Malta,* presents Machiavelli in a prologue which echoes the shock that Christian thinkers had felt, when confronted with Machiavelli's demand that all claims of personal ethics and morality be subordinated to the requirements of the security and survival of the republic.

> *Though some speak openly against my books,*
> *Yet will they read me, and thereby attain*
> *To Peter's chair; and when they cast me off,*
> *Are poison'd by my climbing followers.*
>
> . . . .
>
> *What right had Caesar to his crown?*

Clearly, Machiavelli is here made to stand for an unprincipled belief in personal success of men who ruthlessly climb the ladder to power, including "St. Peter's chair." Such a doctrine is a far cry from Machiavelli's real concern, namely the concern for the state, the *polis,* the *civitas,* which for him, as for the ancients, was the essential prerequisite of all virtue. Only within the political community can men achieve true nobility. Therefore the building and maintaining of the political community becomes a task of primary value. The accomplishment is the condition of all moral conduct and hence cannot in turn be made to depend upon the laws which govern this conduct—an inexorable logic which sounds familiar enough at the present time.

But why revive the ancient verbiage? Why talk about "reason of state," when actually a term such as "constitutional defense" provides so much more convenient an expression? Because, as I hope to show, the concept of the reason of state helps to face the hard core of the issue which such terms as "constitutional defense" and "national interest" tend to obscure. Furthermore, it is in terms of reason of state that the issue has been debated in the past, and some light may be shed upon our present difficulties by the hard-headed reflections of pre-liberal political thought. In doing this, we have to admit, however, that internal and external security get hopelessly mixed up with each other. This was the inclination of all the older writers, usually without any explicit recognition of the fact. In a sense, what we are dealing with here

---

[2] My *Constitutional Reason of State,* Chapter 7.

is the broad issue of "politics and morals." But we are proposing to approach it in terms essentially political rather than moral.[3]

It used to be considered axiomatic that human beings had, by the law of nature, the right to defend themselves. But this proposition was formal, in the sense that it left open the vital question as to how far they might be permitted to go in so defending themselves. Christian doctrine certainly narrowed the scope of the permissible, not only in terms of the "other cheek," but also in those of the older Judaic doctrine of misfortune as a trial sent by God's providence to test a man's steadfastness and moral stamina.

Prevailing thought was to the effect that it was better to endure than to fight back. A passive and patiently suffering role was enjoined upon the good Christian when faced with the aggressor, and more particularly with an oppressive government. Not only to give Caesar what is Caesar's—that might be quite all right—but to give him what he demands without inquiring too closely into his right to demand it, that was seen as the true Christian's proper mode of behavior. It was not only clearly indicated by such sayings as the famous passage in Romans XIII, but also by the actual conduct of countless saints and martyrs.

But there is another strand in the Christian tradition, suggested in the New Testament and amply developed in some of the Church fathers, notably St. Augustine, which sanctions an aggressive conduct in this world's affairs. This contrasting view appears wherever it becomes a question of the defense of the faith and of the communities which live by the faith. Indeed, by the time St. Augustine faced the problems of a Christian Church, the faith had become fully enthroned as the official religion of the Roman Empire, and as a result its defensive assertiveness had become transformed into a recognition that the Church may ask the secular authorities to draw the sword not only in the defense of the faith, but with the intention of spreading it. This is the heart of the Bishop of Hippo's doctrine of the "just war"—a war undertaken to create the conditions for converting the heathens, that is to say, for the spreading of the rule of the Holy Empire. Presumably such a war will be conducted with those means which are customary at the particular time and which are at the disposal of the enemy (including atomic bombs).

This contrasting strand of the Christian teachings which preaches just war in the defense and the spread of the faith raises the issue which became later known as that of the "reason of state" in its most acute form. For reason of state is nothing but the doctrine that whatever is required to insure the

---

[3] Certain broad present-day treatments of this range of issues may be noted here at the outset: Benedetto Croce, *Politics and Morals*, 1945; Reinhold Niebuhr, *Christianity and Power Politics*, 1940; H. Butterfield, *Christianity and History*, 1949; Bertrand de Jouvenel, *Du Pouvoir*, 1947; Ludwig Freund, *Politik und Ethik*, 1955.

survival of the state must be done by the individuals responsible for it, no matter how repugnant such an act may be to them in their private capacity as decent and moral men. Reason of state is merely a particular form of the general proposition that means must be appropriate to the end, must, in other words, be rational in regard to the end, and that those means are the best which are most rational in the sense of being most likely to succeed. But what is truly rational need not be fully clear, let alone self-evident. In any case, "might makes right."

We find Thucydides struggling with this problem in a characteristic way. In the celebrated discussion between the Athenians and the Melians, the Athenians announce the doctrine of the reason of state in no uncertain terms. Might makes right, and "by necessity of their nature, [men] always rule, when they have the power." Justice exists only among equals, and "the powerful exact what they can, while the weak yield what they must." [4] They had argued the same line in an earlier discussion with the Spartans, though in less striking form. There is a clear indication in Thucydides that he thought this bald doctrine of the Athenians one of the causes of their later difficulties. He seems to suggest that the treachery which they encountered was the just dessert of such cynics. But he does not, of course, by arguing thus, abandon his basic preoccupation with reason of state. He merely puts forward the very sensible proposition that a certain amount of pretense, of hypocritical acknowledgment of the values which most members of the community (in this case the Greeks) acknowledge, is part of that "rationality" of means which the doctrine calls for when it enjoins the utmost in exertions on behalf of a given community. Indeed, a moral justification of such hypocrisy may well be argued in some such terms as its value in ensuring survival for a cherished community. But the issue is still relatively easy, when put in terms of patriotism, of the maintenance of an empire, or of a political order which is not itself seen as the essential condition for morality. For an empire is not a moral being in the more elevated sense, which has often, since the ancients, been attributed to the state, and certainly not in the sense in which the Christian Church is.

No one can doubt that, as an organization, a church faces the problem of survival, of a "reason of church." This "reason of church" was most clearly appreciated by the Jesuits. It is a perplexing issue, not usually stated in these terms; those involved in it have well understood the need for camouflage and, better still, of silence. It is natural for anyone in charge of the organization to subordinate the requirements of its survival to individual moral considerations. But suppose the organization itself is believed to be essential for the survival of these moral views? Suppose you are convinced that there can be no Christianity without a Christian Church? And suppose further

---

[4] Thucydides, *Peloponnesian War*, Book V, Chapter 89.

that you believe that the survival of this Church is threatened in the form of rising heretical movements? Then what will be the consequence?

The problems reason of state raises are quite similar. For if the political order is assumed to be an essential condition of a free moral existence, the survival of this order becomes crucial. The old theorists assumed that what was necessary for the security of the state was something not only knowable, but known. To be sure, in their doctrine of the *arcana imperii*, the secrets of empire, of governance, or rule, they recognized that this knowledge was difficult to come by and hidden from the common man.

Thus, there were men, kings and their councillors, who did know these secrets, and who therefore could be expected to act rationally, in terms of these secrets. But does this special knowledge, this insight into the "designs of foreigners" (Locke) really solve the problem of determining what is necessary? Admittedly, those carrying on the work of internal and external security know more than others. But how much more? If we consult the records which are available, such as the British Foreign Office documents of the years before the First World War, or the documents which the U. S. State Department has published by way of apology for its conduct of foreign relations between 1933 and 1939, or the numerous records of security investigations in the United States and elsewhere, we find again and again the same story: the knowledge of the insiders, of the investigators, administrators, and policy makers is woefully inadequate, and certainly did not justify any confidence in their judgment about what constituted the right kind of action, that is to say, the rational road to security and survival.

What is the reason? It is the broad range of contingency in all matters concerning the future course of events, that rulers demand, but without persuasive justification. This contingency is the basis of the kind of appeal typical of all totalitarian movements which says: "Give us the power, and we shall do the rest; don't ask us to explain, we shall take care of you." Free societies are built on the premise that these contingent situations call for broad participation of those affected by them. But this appeal rests on a questionable and exaggerated faith in the rationality of the generality of mankind.[5] It seems more appropriate to stress the unknown and unknowable elements in the contingent nature of political decisions. Such emphasis on the metarational environment provides a basis for a "new belief in the common man," for two reasons. One is that where reason's limit is reached, where a plunge into the unknown is necessary, the will of man is engaged, and this engagement not only should be guided, but will be guided by the "higher"

---

[5] The problem has arisen wherever a constitutional order of the libertarian kind has been confronted with the Communist challenge, and with the Fascist response to that challenge. In England and France, in Italy and Germany, extended debates have been waged over this issue.

rationality of the convictions of the man who acts. The other reason is an expedient one: since men will usually be more willing to accept the consequences of actions which they themselves helped to decide, the participation of all or most men will provide continuity when the consequences of errors are necessitating change. In short, the fact that much of the environment of man is beyond his rational knowledge places strict limitations upon any reason of state.

But the issue as such persists. The problem of security and survival calls for some kind of solution. What shall be the guide, the moral law or the requirements of expediency?

We see this theme all around us in the free world at the present time, though in a secular form. The key value is freedom. There are those who are convinced that the survival of freedom, of a free community, is vitally threatened by the rise of totalitarianism. First the major threat appeared to be the Hitler dictatorship. In the protracted arguments over what to do, the question of war was always involved. Would we Americans be justified, it was asked, in attacking this evil man, this evil organization which threatens our very existence? Or should we even yield to his attacks in order to preserve the peace?

The appeasers won the argument, until the attack took the form of physical aggression upon the United States. Whether it was "the wave of the future" or the "managerial revolution" which served as a basis for the pleading, the underlying notion always was that the United States of America, or Britain, or France was moribund, that in other words the organization was outmoded, was no longer worth defending.

We are in the midst of the argument again at the present time. Quite a few would now argue that it would have been better to resist Hitler at the outset, when he re-armed, when he occupied the Rhineland and so forth, even if they recoil from advocating the desirability of an outright attack, a preventive war. As a result, the United States and her Allies are now pursuing a policy, not of appeasement, but of containment. "Thus far and no farther!" is the battle cry of all those who feel convinced that the survival of the United States of America, and that means her security as well, is decisively bound up with the survival of freedom and justice. We have therefore arrived at the point which St. Augustine saw, and which the Jesuits faced most clearly, although orthodox teachings throughout the intervening years recognized it, too: the point at which there heaves into view the problem of the clash between moral norms for individual life and those requirements of organization which are occasioned by the weapons an enemy is prepared to employ.

This is the issue which is at the heart of all the bitter arguments over civil liberties. The extreme positions are easily grasped and the land resounds with them. On the one hand, there are those who would go to any length to defend the United States against her enemies within and without; on the other hand are those who, regardless of the consequences, would maintain the American belief as embodied in the rights guaranteed by the Constitution. The Republic is being rocked to its very foundations by this controversy. Why? Because the United States, like the churches, is an organization which *rests upon a moral belief*. It is not merely a country that may be right or wrong; its very being is bound up with the maintenance of certain standards. The faith in man which expresses itself in the American Bill of Rights is one without which the United States of America ceases to be what it has been. It may well go on as a people, and probably would, but its essence would be altered, would be revolutionized.

The Communists who maintain this challenge in the modern world are quite frankly believers in a radical rationality of means. Every revolutionary has to be. Karl Marx was quite bland about it. In his opinion, the revolutionary goal of the liberation of the proletariat from its chains was hallowing any means calculated to achieve that end. But for Marx, as for Machiavelli, there was no serious problem involved. Marx, and Lenin following him, was no believer in conventional morality. The individual was for them submerged in the historical process; if he was intelligent and not too much handicapped by class prejudice, he perceived these historical forces and acted accordingly. That is to say, the end did not need to *justify* the means, because the problem of justification only arises when there exists a recognized conception of justice with which the necessary means are in conflict.

For Marx, as for Machiavelli, the approach was rigidly instrumentalist and constructivist. This does not mean that Marx or Machiavelli did not cherish an image of man which transcended the given; quite the contrary. Both believed that in the rightly constructed community, human beings would be morally superior. But this is a projection, something to be achieved in the very process which is the primary concern of these thinkers.[6]

When confronted with the real threat of Communist conquest, the bourgeoisie, so-called, has typically reacted by becoming Fascist. Fascism, though varied in its particular ideological content, has invariably taken the position that any means, even the most inhumane forms of violence, calculated to meet and then to destroy the Communist danger, are "justified." Such brutal expressions as Goering's "where one planes, shavings fall" or Gregor Strasser's "yes, legitimate up to the last rung (of the ladder leading to the gallows), but we still hang them," are characteristic for this outlook.

Similar thought patterns are now common among those who are excited about the Communist danger in the United States. These statements all are basically "reason of state" arguments. The desirability of defending the existing order has come to be taken as self-evident, and hence as a task calling

[6] Cf. James Burnham, *The Machiavellians*, 1943, for a present-day view.

for whatever means are readily at hand. Security and survival are on everyone's lips as the goals in terms of which all political behavior ought to be conducted. The naive surprise with which many editorials nowadays comment upon anyone who questions the total claim made on behalf of security, defense, and survival is very revealing. This remains true, despite rapprochement with the U.S.S.R., on the one hand, or the widespread American disaffection about the undeclared war in Vietnam, on the other.

Is it an accident that the Catholic Church should be so closely associated with these views? Hardly, in the light of history. The church has for many centuries known about the problems involved. As we said, she has been prepared since the days of St. Augustine to take that horn of the dilemma which says that in fighting the enemy all bars are down, that while at war the laws are silent. The Church has been the *Roman* Church, and she carries the heritage proudly. It certainly is a position which has "worked" in a worldly way. Perhaps it is all that can be hoped for.

The United States is, however, basically committed to a position different from that of the Catholic Church. It is committed to a faith in the common man, in the capacity of human beings to work together effectively by granting to each member of the community a substantial amount of freedom, freedom to search out the truth for himself, to argue, and to be wrong. The United States is committed, through its Constitution, to the proposition that we do not know the truth, except in comparative terms. The final truth is there, but no man or group of men can speak with greater assurance about Him than any other. We know that one proposition may contain more truth than another, but we do not know that this proposition is final, and the presumption is that it is not.

For any community built upon such a faith, the task of survival and of security becomes one of defending the *innermost self* as well as that of defending the *outermost boundary*, when confronted with an enemy who manipulates this faith as the Communists do. It is their right, under our assumptions, to claim that their views are more nearly true than ours; but it is not their right to destroy the community which enables them to say so. But how can we stop them from destroying the community? Must we say with Mussolini and Hitler, as well as their latter-day followers, that Communists must be destroyed and that all those who object to their destruction must be destroyed likewise? Must we say that the security and survival of the American community must be achieved, even if it means subverting those very norms and institutions upon which the United States of America rests?

The problem is not peculiar to the United States, though it posits itself here with particular poignancy. The problem has arisen wherever a constitutional order of the libertarian kind has been confronted with the Communist challenge, and with the Fascist response to that challenge. In

England and France, in Italy and Germany extended debates have been waged and certain steps have been taken to try to cope with the situation.[7] What we are here concerned with is a body of thought, of searching political thought which bears upon the issue. It is customary to consider the doctrine of the "reason of state" largely in connection with those writers who in the course of the seventeenth, eighteenth, and nineteenth centuries have been proponents of power, of autocracy and absolutism—Machiavelli and Bodin, Hobbes, Richelieu, Frederick the Great, and Hegel.

But the problem of security and survival faces the constitutional order, faces the government under law, just as much as it does an autocratic government. Hence the deeper thinkers who have developed the political thought of constitutionalism have had to address themselves to this issue. But for them it is a perplexing issue. They were caught in the paradox that we have been discussing. Can you justify the violation of the law, when the survival of the legal order is at stake? These thinkers could not proceed on the easy path of arguing from the supreme value of the state, as could be done by writers such as those above who sanctified order regardless of its justice.

From Machiavelli to Hegel, security and survival of the state and more especially of the good state, of the constitutional, civilized political order, had challenged the ingenuity of the best minds. No clear-cut, definite answer had crystallized by the beginning of the nineteenth century. When constitution-*making* commenced in earnest, those who were framing the new charters tended to fall back upon the Lockean escape into some kind of monarchical prerogative. War powers with its martial law, the state of siege, and so-called emergency powers followed later, often working reasonably well, but at times, as in the case of ill-constructed Article 48 of the Weimar Constitution, wreaking havoc and destroying the very fabric which such powers were meant to preserve.[8]

It was the Nazi destruction of the Weimar Republic and Mussolini's March on Rome that really highlighted the problem of security and survival of a constitutional order in its gravest form, namely, when occurring in the setting of a totalitarian challenge. Not that the problem of internal subversion was novel, even though it had been attenuated in the halcyon days of nineteenth-century liberalism. But internal subversion which seeks to establish another constitutional frame, or which seeks to reestablish an older traditional authoritarian order is not the same deadly threat that totalitarian movements have proved to be. As a consequence, we find con-

---

[7] "Recent Emergency Legislation in West Germany," in *Harvard Law Review,* 82 (1969); cf. also Dieter Sterzel, ed., *Kritik der Notstandsgesetze,* 1968.

[8] Cf. for the most authoritative treatment, Frederick M. Watkins, *The Failure of Constitutional Emergency Powers under the German Republic,* 1939; cf. also C. L. Rossiter's *Constitutional Dictatorship,* 1948.

temporary constitutional systems evolving a variety of new approaches. The threat of total war and total destruction through A-bombs, H-bombs, or bacterial warfare raises even more desperate issues, but little has been done or even proposed to prepare existing constitutional states for such an ordeal.[9]

If we review the thought of the past, we find that the fundamental issue has been answered in a number of ways. Let us restate this fundamental issue once more as follows: how can one, how must one, deal with declared enemies, not only of the established, but of any constitutional order, who yet as citizens are entitled to the protection of the constitution, and more especially are beneficiaries of basic human rights or civil liberties? There are those who would, in line with a long tradition going back to Milton and Calvin, outlaw such persons, deprive them of their status as citizens, and exile or suppress them (put them into camps, perhaps as the McCarran Act[10] proposed to do with Communists and "fellow-travelers" in wartime). There are others who would organize a special tribunal or would entrust an existing one to deal with the task of identifying such elements and of depriving them of some of their liberties.

Emergency powers, that is some species of constitutional dictatorship, have many advocates. There are, however, others who would trust, as Locke had done, to a constitutional order's inherent strength, as long as there is somewhere a "prerogative" of sorts. Still others essentially side with Hegel, thinking that it is all more or less a matter of spiritual force (or some material or biological equivalent thereof), and that nothing much can be done, except to understand these historical forces at work. Finally, there are those who, with Kant, would consider the problem as essentially unresolvable except within the context of an universal order under law, of a constitutionally organized peace that will be "everlasting."

If we glance once more at the historical evolution of the ideas involved, we perceive an interesting pattern. For one, many of the thinkers on constitutional reason of state freely acknowledge their indebtedness to Machiavelli, rather than denouncing him, as was the fashion especially in the seventeenth century. They seem to realize that here was a writer who, whatever his faults and his astigmatism, faced with laudable rigor the problem of security and survival. But although he faced it, he did not really advance it beyond praising the institution of the Roman dictatorship. This was due to his failure to grasp the legal aspect of constitutional government, attached as he was to its libertarian potential.

---

[9] A notable exception is Clinton Rossiter's proposal for a temporary presidential dictatorship of sweeping competence; cf. Rossiter, *Review of Politics*, 9 (1949), 395.

[10] Popularly known as the McCarran Act, this was the Immigration and Nationality Act of 1952, 66 stat. 163.

Three thinkers undertook to develop the Machiavellian heritage in this field, Harrington, Spinoza and Montesquieu. Harrington, with his passion for institutional detail, generalized the Venetian institution of a security council, the dictatorian as he called it, with discretionary powers of ill-defined scope. Spinoza would allow the government all the range of operation which its power would permit it, but insisted upon the rationale of a sphere of individual liberty involved. Montesquieu, troubled by the Roman experience, and facing the despotic potential of contemporary absolutism, believed that a proper amending process could keep the basic law in step with the requirements of the situation, while at the same time he argued for the importance of executive leadership, if suitably restrained by "intermediary powers." This explicitly Machiavellian strand of thought on constitutional reason of state culminated in Hegel, but so did a constrasting strand which is explicitly or implicitly based on the Christian tradition.

Calvin, the Calvinists and Althusius more particularly, conceiving of themselves as "God's people," sanctified the inherent *rationale* of politics by seeing it frankly as the politician's calling. When extended to include the citizen at large, this calling and its rationale become embedded in a concept of emergency powers, to be deployed against tyrants and other subversives, at the discretion of the people's representatives. From here, the road leads to Milton's right of revolution; none of these "warriors of the Lord" have any doubt that the saints will act in accordance with the laws for whose realization they are fighting. The problem of constitutional reason of state is, in a sense, resolved in terms of a transcendent faith in the member of a Christian constitutional community, the "commonweath."

Locke, less sure of the sanctity of the Puritan constituency, but more optimistic about man in general, took refuge in generalizing the traditional English doctrine of the "prerogative." In short, he believed that in every constitutional order fit to survive there must somewhere be someone who can do whatever the emergency situation requires—an outlook still dominant in the United States, since it is inherent in its Constitution.

Rousseau was no constitutionalist, but a democratic absolutist; whatever the general will decides, is right, because rationality is comprehensible only in terms of the general will. But this absolutist reason of state leads to Kant's constitutional form; here the arbitrary will of the collective is once more provided with a rational underpinning in the doctrine of the categorical imperative. This categorical imperative wills the security and survival of the constitutional order; but since the maintenance of law is an essential precondition of the constitutional order itself, the constitutional reason of state wills the scrupulous enforcement of legal rules. However, there remains the external threat and the consequent danger for the maintenance of the constitutional order, as long as no universal constitutional order has been instituted. As a result, the categorical imperative also wills the establishment of such an universal order under law: the achievement of this order is the true constitutional reason of state—to supersede the state by a world constitutionally organized.

The pagan, secular, Machiavellian strand and the Christian and moralist strand are combined into the Hegelian synthesis. For Hegel, the "state" is in the true sense only that part of political organization which is the embodiment of the ethos of a people. The requirements of security and survival of such a state become inherently and necessarily rational. In Hegel's view the actual state most nearly approaching this ideal state is the monarchical constitutional state. History embodies the forward march of the world spirit, and the state is its most potent instrumentality. Hence reason of state, and more especially constitutional reason of state, are given limitless scope to achieve the security and survival of this historically, and hence spiritually, sanctified order. War, far from being a hindrance to this achievement, as in Kant's view, actually turns out to be a necessary tool in the hands of the rulers within a constitutional order as of all other historical orders.

For a free world, faced by the totalitarian challenge, Hegel provides the most radical doctrine of constitutional reason of state. The world spirit who wishes constitutionalism to triumph, because it is the most advanced embodiment of freedom, would sanction any measures required for its victory.

From Machiavelli to Hegel, writers on politics who were tough-minded enough to appreciate the problems of survival, would readily admit that there is no such thing as absolute security. Yet, much contemporary thinking proceeds on this assumption, and an attentive reader of the hearings of congressional bodies will readily discover the extent to which this notion is at work.[11] Against such views, we insist that true security can only be achieved as individual and collective move forward, meeting the challenges as they arise. That is to say, security is not an absolute antithesis to risk, but can only be realized through risk-taking.

Yet a risk to provide a chance for security and survival must be what the military call a "calculated risk." That is to say, it must be related to a weighing of alternatives, alternative roads toward a reasonably well-defined goal. Now, in a sense survival is such a goal, primitive to be sure, but also very basic. Still, survival of a constitutional order involves more than mere self-preservation, because of the rational, the spiritual content of this kind of order. If the maintenance of constitutional freedom, of civil liberties, or

---

[11] Cf., e.g., the hearings entitled *Commission on Government Security*, held before a Senate Subcommittee on Reorganization of the Committee on Government Operations, 1955.

basic rights [12] is implicit in the goal of survival, then their suppression becomes paradoxical.

We cannot retreat with Hegel into the cloudy and mystical realm of the world spirit and its undisclosed workings. A rational solution of this problem in constitutional terms imposes itself as the very essence of constitutional reason of state. It is going to involve the taking of calculated risks; without risks, there can be no security, hence the paradoxical confusion of the term "security risk" to designate a person who is wanted for the security of the constitutional order, although or indeed *because* he is a risk, but a risk worth taking.

Within the framework of this range of ideas, certain approaches to the problem in the constitutional and administrative practice of our times might be more fruitfully examined. The particular way in which England and France, Italy and Germany, as well as some of the smaller nations of Europe, have sought to deal with the problem of security might be profitably juxtaposed to present trends in the United States. It is my belief that something more promising can reasonably be advocated as a viable solution to the problems of security and survival than has so far been embodied into the law of any of the existing constitutional systems.

Here it might be interesting, though, to cast a fleeting glance at the diversity of solutions attempted in several present-day constitutional systems. For there is extraordinary variety, and the reasons for this variety are not, at the moment, very clear unless it be the difficulty and complexity of the issues involved. Whether any of these solutions really are viable, only experience can tell. A theoretical analysis certainly would leave one very much in doubt. For until now, those constitutional systems which survived, did so not because they had solved the problem of internal security, but because the problem never became sufficiently serious in the liberal age to threaten the existence of these states. Others which perished, notably the constitutions of Italy (1926), Germany (1933), and Czechoslovakia (1948), had not made what one could describe as adequate efforts even at solving the problem. It is these experiences which have, as a matter of fact, lent poignancy to the search for an answer in our day. The catastrophies of Italy, Germany, and Czechoslovakia continue to stir the imagination to seek a more effective solution to the problem. Needless to add, the failure of younger nations to implant constitutionalism as opposed to more arbitrary governmental form also challenges our ingenuity.

There are today roughly four major modes of approaching the issue of constitutional defense, i.e., of internal constitutional reason of state. The first approach to the problem is to outlaw, by legislation, a party or

---

[12] On the evolution of the American constitutional semantics from rights to liberties to freedom, I gave some brief hints in "Rights, Liberties, Freedoms," 1942.

organization that is engaged in efforts to undermine or destroy the constitutional order and to establish a different and nonconstitutional one. This legislative method of solving the problem is found in the United States and Switzerland, with the American legislature slightly restrained by the judicial power of review. The second approach also provides for outlawry of the subversive group or organization, but by way of a judicial decision, made upon request of the executive; such decision may make the organization illegal or it may deprive the members of the organization in question of certain basic rights, specifically mentioned in the constitution. This is the method employed in the German Federal Republic. The third approach is through the elimination of presumed subversives from defined positions in the administrative services, both private and public, either by administrative regulation or by legislation. This administrative method of dealing with the problem is found in France and in Italy, but also to a considerable extent in the United States. Characteristically, the administrative measures are restrained, but at the same time also sanctioned, by an administrative court, such as the *Conseil d'Etat,* or by an administrative commission, such as the president's loyalty board.

The fourth mode is to develop detailed legislation for eliminating the characteristic practices of such a subversive or totalitarian group or organization, rather than outlawing the group itself. This method is illustrated by Britain's Public Order Act of 1936; it is also found in many states of the United States. There is at present a wholesome tendency to develop this approach elsewhere, through suitable revisions of the penal law, e.g., in France and the German Federal Republic.

Constitutional reason of state is, I hope to have shown, in the last analysis a matter of ever more effectively ordering a "government of laws." Three hundred years ago, in the great English Revolution fought and won for the idea of constitutional liberty, Oliver Cromwell perhaps felt more deeply than any other before or since, the dialectic that the security and survival of such an order posits. Cromwell had despaired of getting his countrymen to adopt such a constitutional order of their own free will. But there is something which he knew and he told his several parliaments: that "in every government, there must be somewhat fundamental, somewhat like a *Magna Charta,* that should be standing and be unalterable. . . ." And he knew also that among these fundamentals, the most fundamental of all is the right of a man to his conviction, his belief, his faith. For here is the hard core of man's dignity. To make his innermost self secure is more vital to the security and survival of a constitutional order than any boundary or any secret. It is the very core of constitutional reason of state. It is the reason why a constitutional state is founded and is maintained.

ADMINISTRATION AND CONSTITUTIONAL- ISM

8

For forms of government let fools contest;
Whatever is best administered is best.[1]

In these lines, Alexander Pope expressed a contempt for the preoccupation of constitutionalists. He stated a concern with practical results and has been quoted again and again in works on administration and the mercantilists.[2] The problem of conducting government rationally had come to be seen more in the workaday doings of the administrators who built roads and dams, organized manufactures, and provided hospitals. They attended to the hundred and one tasks of communal concern rather than to the moral dilemmas of foreign policy and other high matters of state. Immorality had yielded to amorality. Technical necessity had replaced the "mysteries of state." Policies were the task of the police, and the police had their finger in everything. To this day the "building-police" in European cities reminds us of this expansion of administrative responsibility and discretion. The rapid widening of the net of police power in the United States offers a contemporary analogy.[3] It is part of this development that constitutions everywhere are being called upon to limit and restrain such overgrowth of governmental activities.

The public at large is inclined to favor the good administrator over the loyal constitutionalist. Discretion is king. Discretion, in the English tradition, is closely related to the prerogative of the king. It is not only a problem in constitutionalism, but in all law-making.

What is discretion? Discretion may be defined in various ways, but

[1] Alexander Pope, *Essay on Man*, Ep. 3.

[2] Eli F. Heckscher, *Mercantilism*, 1935.

[3] O. W. Wilson, *Police Administration*, 1950, and James Q. Wilson, "The Police and Their Problems: A Theory," 1963.

however defined, it usually involves (1) a choice between alternative courses of action; and (2) that such a choice not be made arbitrarily, wantonly, or carelessly, but in accordance with the requirements of the situation. The concept of discretion usually also involves a framework of rules within which it comes into play. Discretion in short is needed whenever no specific rules or principles can be or have been established, yet a decision has to be made. It is intended to avoid mere whim and to substitute responsible conduct.

Such responsible conduct beyond the law raises a very serious problem whenever damage results from it. The ancient rule that "the king can do no wrong" caused the individual administrator to be held responsible for such damage. This rule means that the government cannot be held liable for acts committed by an official in the discharge of his duty. Damage suits against officials must, therefore, always establish that the official acted *ultra vires,* that is, beyond what he was legally authorized to do. If the court finds he acted *ultra vires,* the claim has to be enforced against the individual officer.

It is evident that in many cases the individual officer is quite unable to pay the claim. If, on the other hand, the court finds that the official did not act *ultra vires,* then the damaged party is dependent upon the grace of a "sovereign legislature" for adequate compensation. The disadvantages of this situation are, however, by no means limited to the "public" which may sustain damages. Inasmuch as it exposes the official to constant danger of a ruinous suit for personal damages, it makes him overly cautious and thus irresponsible, because he fails to pursue his duties vigorously.

The recognition of this exceedingly unsatisfactory state of affairs has led legislative bodies to provide specifically for the responsibility of certain large-scale government enterprises in the case of torts committed by any of its officials. Certain municipalities have recognized their obligation for damage done by their fire departments, and the federal government has provided similarly in the case of the TVA. It is indeed as evident as anything can be that the government should take the same responsibility for any large-scale service enterprise it manages as would be provided for if that enterprise were privately owned and operated. If it is to the community's benefit to undertake such tasks, the community and not the damaged individual should bear the losses involved in its operation.

Actual experience in local government bodies where a certain amount of that type of corporate liability is allowed tends to show that objectively responsible conduct in terms of the particular service can be secured by internal measures. Policies, like laws, cannot be made sufficiently detailed to fit all situations, and therefore must leave much to the discretion of those who execute them. In dangerous emergency situations, the legislator may grant considerable leeway to those in charge. War usually entails such grants; they were made in the United States and Britain, although the policy maker, e.g., the Congress, may retain the right to suspend or annul such discretionary acts. In any case, it is clear that discretion is inherent in effective administration, even though often in conflict with constitutionalism. Constitutional limitations of the exercise of power, its restraints, and more particularly its guarantee of human rights are apt to clash with administrative efficiency.

Even so, constitutionalism is not a much discussed subject in studies on administration, not even by the broadest approaches to this subject. This disinclination to consider constitutionalism a vital aspect of administration is in part due to the "behavioral" approach to political science, with its belittling of institutional aspects of political life. It is also due to the declining belief in the significance of constitutional forms which are seen as "merely formal," although it is impossible to gain a realistic perspective on the behavior of American administrators without taking the constitutional context into account. Their everyday dependence upon Congress and the judiciary are patent evidence of the role of constitutionalism in all mature democratic systems of the West, Britain as much as the United States, and the Scandinavian countries and Belgium as much as France and Switzerland. The slogan of "responsible bureaucracy" is the expression relating administration to constitutionalism.[4]

Let us elaborate briefly this issue of responsibility. There often occur situations in politics where an actor, R, is supposed to render an account of his actions to another actor, A. Strictly speaking, he is accountable. Accountability is a special form of responsibility. A responsible administrator would be such an actor R. One might wish that we knew more about the various modes of enforcing such responsibility. Besides dismissal of the official, five ways of enforcement have been identified: disciplinary measures, promotional techniques, financial measures of control, judicial measures, and technical training and the resulting sense of craftsmanship. Basically, responsibility has two facets, one personal, the other technical and functional; that is to say, an A may be responsible to another, R, or he may be responsible in terms of a certain standard of purpose. It is clear that responsibility cannot be separated from power, whether formal, informal, or merely influence. The question of whether a person acts responsibly or not necessarily involves the question of how much discretion he can exercise; for where there is no discretion, no responsibility can exist.

Discretion comes into play whenever no rules or principles can be or have been formulated and at the same time mere arbitrary whim cannot be allowed. Consider the choice of personnel. A legislative body or a governor

---

[4] See my (with Taylor Cole) *Responsible Bureaucracy—A Study of the Swiss Civil Service*, 1932; Charles Hyneman, *Bureaucracy in a Democracy*, 1950; John Millett, *Government and Public Administration: The Quest for Responsible Performance*, 1959. See also O. Glenn Stahl, *Public Personnel Administration*, 6th ed., 1971. For an overview, cf. R. K. Merton, ed., *Reader in Bureaucracy*, 1952.

may give fairly precise rules and establish firm regulations for the selection of personnel as is done in civil service legislation. Yet there will usually remain an element of discretionary choice. The candidates may all be of a certain age, may all have a certain education and experience and come from certain localities, and may possess a variety of other specified traits. At times the candidates may be identical in all these respects, and yet a choice has to be made among them. The selection committee may have to decide whether to prefer a man from Yale or from Harvard, and they may have to evaluate the exact meaning of the words used in the letters of recommendation and so forth.

Law or custom may then give the selection committee discretion in selecting the candidate. The expectation will be that the persons invested with such discretion will use it "to the best of their ability." It means that they will give careful thought to all the factors involved in the choice. They may evaluate the writers of the letters of recommendation, consider their reliability, and their past record as recommenders. The selecting committee may also feel that there are already several Harvard men in the organization and that there should be some diversity, or they may feel that on account of the good experience with Yale men, preference should be given to another Yale man. They will be troubled, if a member of the committee seems to harbor certain prejudices, either for certain men or against others, let alone to engage in personal favoritism. Such favoritism may border on corruption, as, for example, when it is found that judges appointed by a certain governor have been very generous in making contributions to party campaigns.

It generally will be assumed that a person vested with power to exercise discretion will be able to give reasons for what he has done. This aspect is particularly evident where a superior gives a subordinate discretion. He will ordinarily assume that the subordinate will use good sense, experience, stick to established precedent, and so on. But he will also expect the subordinate to be able to "explain," if for any reason he finds that the decision made ought to be subjected to review. The superior will rarely be satisfied with an explanation such as "I just felt that way" or "my instinct told me this was the right man," let alone an explanation which would say "I liked his face" or "she had such a lovely voice." Among these grounds for reasoned elaborations of the discretionary decision arrived at, constitutional provisions will often play an important role, for many values and beliefs are fixed in the constitution and the reference to it will be beyond discussion. "We cannot do this, because it would be unconstitutional" will under constitutionalism be considered a definitive argument.

If one examines such "reasoned elaboration" or inquires into what is expected under such a heading, he finds that the reasoning involved proceeds to argue both in terms of means and ends. The personnel man may suggest that the person chosen believes in democracy, or he may insist that the man rejected is possibly a believer in socialism or is a fellow traveler. He may say that the candidate is steady and a good family man, or reversely that he is a drunkard and a bachelor. But besides such value judgments, there may be instrumental judgments, dwelling upon the man's ability, his knowledge of foreign languages, or what have you. The discretion as used is, in other words, tied to the opinions, values, and beliefs shared by members of the organization, as well as to the tasks to be performed.

It is by now becoming apparent why discretion is so valuable and indeed also why it is so inescapable an aspect of not only all government and administration, but all human relationships. Philosophers have since time immemorial dwelt upon the fact that rules can never cope with the infinite variety and detail of the concrete situations. To cope with the resulting inadequacy of all law, they have at times sought to find persons of exceptional wisdom, to identify as it were a natural elite of persons who would be so wise as to be able to exercise limitless discretion. Plato went perhaps further than any other thinker in this respect, at least the younger Plato of the *Republic.* Nor is it easy to argue against him, once the crucial concession is made that such men can be found by some reliable method. Plato himself took refuge in the hope of some kind of providential coincidence by which the philosopher and the holder of absolute power are brought together. Most of the rest of us have rejected his notion of the philosopher-king, precisely because the problem that he minimized, namely how to find the persons worthy of being entrusted with so much discretion, seems to be the most difficult.[5]

In the choice of personnel, as our humble illustration suggested, some of the most persistent discretionary problems present themselves. But though one rejects Plato's notion of a natural elite, and most of what goes with it, the fact remains that precisely where the novel, unprecedented situation arises, calling for creative innovation and invention, all rules and regulations break down, and discretion comes to the fore. And when such discretion is used in such a way as to benefit society, when, as the ancient verbiage has it, the "general good" is served, then government and administration are most universally acclaimed. Eisenhower deciding to cross the channel, Congress deciding to grant Puerto Rico commonwealth status, Truman deciding to act in Korea, Kennedy facing down Khrushchev in the missile crisis—these are instances of the exercise of discretion in dramatic situations calling for creative initiative and were utterly removed from the possibility of being handled by precedent or established rule.

Whenever discretion is thus used, whenever the factors relevant to a

---

[5] Cf. Plato, *Republic,* especially at 473 d. Aristotle, dubious of this doctrine, has an approach to the problem of discretion which is more nearly in keeping with our views, especially in connection with his doctrine of *epieikeia.* Cf. my *Philosophie des Rechts,* 1954, Chapter 2.

decision are obviously numerous and at least in part unforeseeable, it will seem to most men that an attempt to limit such discretion by pre-established rule or regulation would be unwise and in its consequences probably unjust, perhaps even disastrous. But it appears similarly unwise and unjust to entrust such discretionary power to persons not qualified to exercise good judgment, that is to say, not acting in such a way that their reasoning could afterwards be examined and found defensible. At this point, we are confronting the vital relationship of discretion to responsibility. Irresponsible discretion is not what is ordinarily wanted. But what constitutes "responsible discretion?" Essentially it is discretion that is exercised with due regard to all the considerations that enter into the situation. This will usually mean that the person exercising such discretion is duly qualified. He will seem to act responsibly when he acts in accordance with the full knowledge of the particular science, art, craft, or operation involved in the situation calling for discretion. That is why the selection of personnel appears as the core of the problem of how to arrange for the exercise of discretion. And that is why administrative responsibility turns to such a large extent upon evaluation of the performance in terms of objective standards prevalent in a particular field of work and the sense of workmanship connected with it.[6]

At this point, the relation of discretion to the rational aspect of authority becomes almost self-evident. When a person possesses the capacity to act in such a way that his communications concerning his actions possess by implication the potentiality of being supported by effective reasoning, he would appear to be eminently suited to occupy a position of discretionary power. The exercise of discretionary power presupposes the possession of authority. Whenever a person possesses authority, in the sense in which we have been employing the term, he is capable of using discretion. The fact that his decisions, commands, or other communications could be reinforced by reasoned elaboration relating them to established values and beliefs will lend his acts that "authority" without which discretion becomes arbitrary abuse of power.[7]

Among the sources of authority, a constitution is a very important one. Present-day constitution-making is often stimulated by the fact that the authority of those who try to govern a country can be reinforced by such a constitution. Such authority is linked to legitimacy, and in the next chapter the legitimizing effect of constitutionalism will be examined. For the issue of a constituent power is in a sense the touchstone of operative constitutionalism. Here it must suffice to stress that through its performing well, as

---

[6] Cf. my *Constitutional Government and Democracy*, 4th ed., 1968, Chapter 19, and *The New Belief in the Common Man*, 1941, Chapter 6, "Responsibility and the Sense of Workmanship." Cf. the works cited in footnote 10.

[7] For the use of authority in this sense, cf. my *Tradition and Authority*, 1972, Chapter 6 and the literature cited there.

shown by results, a bureaucracy can contribute significantly to legitimation of a particular regime, and more especially to a constitutional order.

In any case, the constitution provides the basis for authoritative administration. In a very real sense, it offers that reasoned elaboration for an administrative decision which is recognized as the quintessence of authority. When there is good reason for doing or believing something, such action or thought acquires a quality which is otherwise lacking; it becomes "authoritative." [8] Much Anglo-American legal tradition has retained the Stoic presumption that reason is of decisive importance in providing law with the necessary authority. [9] The reasoning is that of "men learned in the law," that is to say, judges. Administration cannot hope to be authoritative, unless through an appeal to law it is provided with reasoned elaboration.

Against such a view, it is often held, particularly among administrators, that the authority of him who wields power consists in "blind" obedience to his commands. It follows that the more blind the obedience, the more authoritative is the powerholder. As a result, authority is viewed with suspicion, if not condemned outright, and not only the writings of the anarchists provide many illustrations. [10] But authority seen as the capacity of reasoned elaboration demonstrates that authority is not measured by blind obedience, but by the degree of persuasiveness that inheres in a given command. The citizen and the subordinate who have been led to comprehend the reasons for the command are subject to authority, but it is the genuine authority of reasoned elaboration. Constitutional regimes have the constitution by which to effectuate such elaboration. The values and beliefs upon which it rests are those prevalent in the political community; administration that proceeds in accordance with the constitution is thereby made more effective.

An interesting recent illustration of the range of issues involved is provided by certain modern techniques, such as wiretapping. Obviously, such a practice gives the police and other law-enforcing agencies means for discovering conspiracies and other criminal activities. The courts have been called upon to limit these practices by examining their constitutionality. The controversy continues, but the fact of subjecting these techniques to constitutional scrutiny has enhanced their effectiveness by clothing them with authority. From these contextual features arises the view that constitutionalism is needed for the advanced industrial society, and hence will

[8] Cf. my *The Philosophy of Law in Historical Perspective*, 2nd ed., 1963c, especially Chapters 2, 4, 6, 8, 11, 13, and 14.

[9] Sir Edward Coke, *Reports*, Vol. 12, p. 65; my *Man and His Government*, 1963b, Chapter 10.

[10] Cf. Chapter 12 in my *Man and His Government*, and Volume 1 of *Nomos*, 1958.

advance in such developing societies, which at the start for reasons of short-run efficiency, adopted nonconstitutional systems.

It is therefore unfortunate that some scholars have commenced to speak of such regimes as "authoritarian." For, to be sure, authority is enhanced by subjecting governmental agencies to processes of reasoned elaboration for their decisions and administrative measures. The issues here touched would lead too far afield; it suffices to have stressed the point that administration is linked to constitutionalism through the need for authority in the sense here employed. This is particularly important, because the technicity of modern administration carries with it the threat of totalitarian abuse of force, and hence the move toward totalitarianism.[11] That the latter offers short-run advantages for the "efficient" administrator is clear. But whether in planning and programming or in other fields, these advantages are short-run and likely to turn into lethal defects in course of time.[12]

In conclusion, we might state once more that Pope's famous lines are confusing the issue. For the forms of government over which men contest are not a foolish issue in the perspective of the quality of administration. For these forms of government, and more especially the constitutional divergencies between them, profoundly affect the quality of administration. It is in the interest of this quality that men contest over the issue of constitutionalism and its implications.[13]

[11] See my (with Z. Brzezinski), *Totalitarian Dictatorship and Autocracy*, 1967, Chapters 1, 2, and 16.

[12] My *Totalitarian Dictatorship and Autocracy*, note 14, Chapter 28.

[13] When bureaucracy is faced by anarchy, it needs inspirational leadership; cf. my Clark Memorial lecture, published in the journal *Canadian Public Administration*, (1970), under the title "Bureaucracy Faces Anarchy."

LEGITIMACY AND CONSTITUTIONAL-ISM

IN THE NAME OF THE PEOPLE?

9

The French Revolution posed the question of legitimacy in concrete terms. Rousseau had raised it in the famous opening sentences of his *Contrat Social:* "Man is born free and everywhere he is in chains. One thinks himself the master of others, and still remains the greater slave than they. How did this change come about? I do not know. What can make it legitimate? That question I think I can answer." [1] His answer was that the general will of the people is the only ground of legitimacy; for only they can say who has the right to rule them.

Legitimate rule is rightful rule, and many specific grounds have been believed in the course of the evolution of government. Constitutionalism has been the modern ground: only a regime or rule which is based upon the will of the people is legitimate. To put it another way: the constitution-making power, the constituent power of the people provides legitimate government. By the middle of the twentieth century the prevalent claim to legitimacy is democratic legitimacy. The constituent power is believed to be constitutionalist. Even the totalitarian regimes of this century have claimed to be thus based upon the will of the people. The constitution of the Soviet Union starts with this claim: "All power in the U.S.S.R. belongs to the working people of town and country as represented by the Soviets of Working People's Deputies" (Art. 3). The decisive qualification in this statement is of course the adjective "working"; for only those who work are said to be truly a part of the people.

Legitimacy has been a favored hunting ground for political and partisan propaganda. The term became current as a slogan with the controversies leading to and away from the French Revolution. Rousseau's

[1] Rousseau, *Le Contrat Social,* 1762.

stress on the *will* of the people called forth a radical reaction both in traditionalist and rationalist terms. Burke proclaimed immemorial custom the basis of the prescriptive right of the constitution; [2] de Maistre argued divine right in terms of alleged Catholic doctrine; [3] and many others followed with arguments all of which amounted to saying that rule, unless legitimate, was bad and then, insistently, that some particular belief was the true ground of legitimacy, and hence the only ground on which title to rule, legitimate rule, could be claimed. A major effort at systematizing the many grounds upon which claims to legitimacy, that is to say titles to rule, may be based was made by Max Weber. He unfortunately failed to distinguish legitimacy from authority which confuses the argument.

From what has so far been said, it is clear that legitimacy can be achieved only when there exists a prevalent belief as to what provides a rightful title to rule. If the community is basically divided on this matter, then no legitimacy is possible. This is at times connected with what the Greeks called *anomie*, that is to say a state of mind in the community when no *nomos*, no prevalent notions concerning what is right, exist any longer.[4] But although often observed, and especially in the Athenian *polis* of Plato's day, this connection does not always exist. It is possible for a community to be basically divided on much of what constitutes right, yet to have a prevalent belief as to what constitutes a good title to rule, as was the case in the period of the religious wars in Europe, when blood descent and symbolic representation of God on earth were generally accepted as good titles to monarchical rule.[5] It is also possible for a community to be basically agreed on most of what constitutes right, yet to be split on its belief as to what constitutes legitimate rule, as happened in France recently and prior to de Gaulle's assumption of power.

De Gaulle's opting for democratic constitutionalism reestablished the legitimacy of this type of rule because of the authority which de Gaulle could bring to it.[6] From these situations it follows that a division in the political community on what constitutes legitimacy must be distinguished from general *anomie*, even though it has a relation to it. Furthermore, it is very important to draw a clear distinction between the absence of any

[2] Burke, "Speech on Representation," May 7, 1782, in *Works*, Vol. V, p. 405.

[3] De Maistre, *Du Pape*, 1843, p. 255; also pp. 168 ff.

[4] Cf. my *Man and His Government*, 1963b, Chapters 10, 12 and 13. Emile Durkheim, *De la Division du Travail Social*, 1893; Sebastian de Grazia, *The Political Community*, 1948.

[5] Karl Löwenstein, *Die Monarchie im Modernen Staat*, 1952, pp. 175 ff.

[6] See my "The New French Constitution in Political and Historical Perspective," 1959, and Nicholas Wahl, "Aux Origines de la nouvelle constitution," 1950.

cherished standards and value judgments (*anomie*) and the presence of clearly defined divergences in such standards and judgments.[7]

What then, one might ask at this point, is legitimacy? To what phenomenon does legitimacy refer? It is a very particular kind of consensus which concerns the question of the right or title to rule or to govern. Such right we have seen to be founded upon a variety of beliefs. The magical belief in "descent from the gods," manifest in supernatural powers of the ruler, has been widespread. From the primitive tribal kings and priests described by anthropologists [8] to the "son of heaven" in Chinese imperial rule we have this sort of legitimacy. Another widespread ground has been the belief in blood descent which assimilates the right to rule to the right of property; Western monarchy clearly illustrates this title. The notion that the ruler resembles God on earth as the symbol of divine rule has been linked with both these older notions as an important ground of legitimacy. But it is difficult to say whether the institution of monarchy has engendered the belief in monotheism or vice versa; at any rate the two beliefs have reinforced each other.

Finally, the fact that a certain kind of rule has been exercised for a considerable length of time and that it corresponds to prevalent custom or tradition has served to provide it with legitimacy. Whereas these notions relate to an individual ruler, they apply also to a constitution, especially tradition. Its believed-in legitimacy has more typically been based upon an expression of preference on the part of those subject to it. When accepted by a referendum or at least by popularly elected representatives in a constituent assembly, such legitimacy seems assured.

A curious case occurred at the time of American military government after the Second World War in Germany. When constitutions had been drafted in the several *Laender* (states) of the American zone of occupation, Americans preferred that these drafts be submitted to popular referendum, and they eventually insisted upon it. Germans felt that such a referendum was meaningless, since the German electorate had no well-defined notions concerning the issues involved. The issue came to a head in the state of Hesse where the draft contained provisions for a certain amount of socialization of private property (banks, insurance, etc.). The American military governor, General Lucius D. Clay, wanted these provisions taken out and submitted in a separate referendum, arguing that the voter ought not to be forced to accept such provisions if he wanted

---

[7] See my *The New Belief in the Common Man*, 1941, Chapter 5, for further detail on the application of this principle to democracy; cf. also Christian Bay, *The Structure of Freedom*, 1958, for a striking discussion of the relation of this issue to that of freedom. See my *Man and His Government*, Chapters 20 and 21.

[8] A. L. Kroeber, *Anthropology*, rev. ed., 1948; J. G. Frazier, *The New Golden Bough*, ed. T. H. Gaster, 1959.

to approve the rest of the constitution. The German Socialist leader pointed out to the American general that there was no need for this, since the majority would do what the party and its leaders told them to do. "If I urge them to accept these provisions, they will do so, whether in a separate document or not." In the sequel, although the provisions were approved by the referendum, little has been done since to implement them. This particular case shows that the legitimizing effect of popular votes by majority is not limited to particular rulers or regimes, but extends to constitutional rules.

The question of legitimacy must not be confused with that of legality, though under certain circumstances the distinction is not easy to draw. The legality of a rule is the result of its being in accordance with the positive law; it may therefore be the same as legitimacy, when the prevalent belief merely asks that the title to rule be in accordance with the law in order for it to be considered legitimate. Here it might be said that legalism is itself an ideology justifying rule. A special form of this type of legitimacy would be the belief that merely a certain measure of "rule of law" legitimizes a government, as some lawyers might hold.

Yet there have been many situations in which perfect legality of a given rule did not provide legitimacy, for example, the rule of Louis XVI in France in 1789. The ground of belief having shifted, the rightfulness of the rule, the belief in it among those subject to it, had disappeared. Conversely, in all those situations where a ruler abuses his power, breaking the law, the question of his legitimacy in doing so is distinct from that of legality. It may be perfectly legitimate, if believed to be in accordance with some generally held belief.

In post-revolutionary situations, the new regime may lack a full legitimacy. Then the new regime may seek to improve its situation by so-called plebiscites in which the people are asked to approve what the rulers have done, e.g. the plebiscites Napoleon Bonaparte held in France or those of Hitler and de Gaulle in our time. Although often manipulated and hence a fraud, they do not fail to impress the populace and foreign powers.[9] Constitutional and unconstitutional regimes alike may be legitimized, and it is clear that the constitution therefore does not only legitimize but also stands itself in need of legitimacy. The persons who are partisans of a constitutional regime and have succeeded in instituting it, usually in the sequel to a revolution, have been called the constituent power—a power not within but outside and transcending the constitutional order. There tends to be a residuary and unorganized power of resistance in the political community and this constituent power can only come into play when

---

[9] See for such plebiscites my (with Z. Brzezinski) *Totalitarian Dictatorship and Autocracy*, rev. ed., 1965, Chapter 13.

the government fails to function satisfactorily, especially after lost wars.

In light of what has so far been said, an acceptable classification of types of legitimacy would be the religious, the juristic (philosophical), the traditional, and the procedural. The religious types would presumably relate to the several religions and their distinctive notions about rule and rulership, such as the Christian, the Confucian, the Mohammedan, and so forth; the juristic of philosophical types would refer to the several conceptions of forms of government and would therefore parallel the types of rule; the traditional ones would do the same, but not in terms of a belief based upon philosophical reasoning, but upon custom. In fact, in any strict sense, the traditional forms of legitimacy are not really distinct, but implement the religious and philosophical ones. Procedural types are the notions relating the elections of various kinds, especially the democratic legitimacy of a majority vote.

But there is still another and quite universal ground of legitimacy which I should like to call performance legitimacy or success legitimacy. Success in war, and the maintenance of prosperity, order, and peace are important ingredients. The legitimizing effect of good performance is great, and the decline in legitimacy as a result of failure has been important in the operation of democratic regimes. When people started to talk about the "credibility gap" resulting from the war in Vietnam, the legitimacy both of the president and of the Constitution were jeopardized. Democratic legitimacy in modern constitutional regimes is subject to continuous performance tests, especially in the economic realm; the original legitimacy of a newly elected government may be broadened or narrowed by the performance achieved in its operation.

Performance as a ground of legitimacy is purely pragmatic, and, as such, radically different from the religious ground. In Western history, the religious ground was prevalent in the Middle Ages. Medieval constitutionalism evolved in response to the changing attitude toward the church. The church and secular government both claimed divine sanction, and a protracted struggle was fought over whether the divine sanction of the secular government was direct, a claimed by Charlemagne and many of his successors on the Imperial throne, as well as the kings of England, France, and Spain, or whether it was derived from ecclesiastical consecration. Charlemagne proclaimed that he was crowned by God, but nonetheless sought papal affirmation of his right to rule. Eventually, in the high Middle Ages, Thomas Aquinas stressed the difference between a legitimate ruler and a tyrant, insisting that only a ruler who governed according to law was legitimate, and thereby introducing the criteria of performance and the relationship to constitutionalism. In doing so, he called Aristotle to record in support of a "mixed government" in which power is divided according to a constitution. Hence medieval constitutionalism provided a nearly secular ground of legitimacy, a rational ground for which the constitution rested upon ancient custom and tradition as well as philosophical understanding. The most radical statement of this view was offered by Marsilius of Padua in the generation after Thomas Aquinas; the consent of the people (aristocratically defined) becomes the basis of legitimacy.[10]

A modern secular version of religious legitimacy is the stress laid by some writers on agreement on fundamentals (and on ideology). The "agreement on fundamentals" as a necessary prerequisite of political order has haunted political theory since the days of Plato and Aristotle. Whatever was right for the Greek *polis*, the situation of the great modern states with their millions of people is radically different. Dissent is needed for the maintenance of intellectual and cultural, as well as political vitality. Far from presupposing an "agreement on fundamentals," as writers from Burke to Laski have argued, constitutional democracy has achieved political order in diversity and has managed to organize decision-making in spite of *disagreement* on fundamentals. The argument has, of course, a semantic aspect since much depends upon what is understood by fundamentals. As commonly understood, such fundamentals would certainly comprise religion, culture, and views on the economy and its organization. Regarding all *these* fundamentals, the greatest diversity has characterized such polities as Great Britain and the Dominions, the United States, and Switzerland. Fundamentals may generally be taken to be basic beliefs or convictions which provide the starting point for all discussion on actions to be taken—propositions that cannot be further analyzed and hence provide a foundation.

The issue of legitimacy shows, however, that there ought indeed to be a *measure* of agreement on one fundamental, and that is the kind of rule that is right and the sort of ruler who is entitled to rule. In a democracy, this question will be settled in a constitution (written or unwritten), and the acceptance of the "rules of the game" laid down in the constitution will be the one basic agreement required. As such a constitution typically embodies basic human freedoms, including more particularly the freedom of self-expression, the basic agreement may also paradoxically be called the agreement to disagree.[11] Sixteenth-century writers, like Johannes Althusius, who lay great stress on *concordia*, that is to say consensus, are in a way

---

[10] See my *Philosophy of Law in Historical Perspective*, 2nd ed., 1963, Chapter 6, and *Transcendent Justice*, 1964, Chapter 2. The decisive reference to Aristotle's *Politics* is found in *Summa Theologica*, Book 2, Part 1, question 95, article 4. See also Dolf Sternberger on legitimacy in the *International Encyclopedia*, and my *Man and His Government*, Chapter 13, footnote 4.

[11] See footnote 7, above.

demonstrating the transition from religious to secular legitimacy; for such *concordia* is at once employed as a reason for religious conformity and as a reason for agreeing on the fundamentals of government.

If legitimacy can be achieved only when there exists a prevalent communal belief as to rightful rule, it follows that there may be political conditions under which legitimacy is not possible. Such conditions are usually felt to be undesirable, for the good reason that it is helpful for a government to be legitimate. We are face to face with a primary proposition regarding legitimacy, namely, that legitimate rule is more effective rule, other things being equal, than nonlegitimate rule.[12]

A distinctive pattern of legitimacy, not to be confused with the typical totalitarian ideology, is that provided by modern nationalism. More especially in the newly emerging political orders, but already in the national unification and liberation movements in Europe (Italy, Germany, Poland, and the Austrian succession states), the most potent source of legitimacy was effectiveness in forwarding the freedom of the emergent nation. Political figures as divergent as Bismarck and Cavour, Masaryk and Pilsudski, Bolivar, and the host of their equals in contemporary Asia and Africa all derive the legitimacy of their rule from their effectiveness in liberating and uniting the group that finds itself as a nation in the nascent political world order. It is frequently impossible to determine whether the leader legitimizes the nation, or the nation the leader. The right to rule emerges in the interaction between the two, often in the course of violent sanguinary conflict, as for example, in Algeria.

All forms of legitimizing rule in terms of popular preferences, whether defined broadly by ideologies or narrowly by such goals as prosperity, security, or national freedom, are characteristic of an egalitarian outlook on legitimacy. This outlook is preoccupied not with what intrinsic capacity men have to govern, but with what performance they are able to offer. The "capacity" is relegated to the "lower" echelons of administrative personnel who are expected to demonstrate "merit" through elaborate examinations based upon long training and/or experience. At this point, the kinship between the democratic and bureaucratic outlook is patently demonstrated. Their joint emphasis contrasts sharply with the aristocratic view, as well as with its assorted "elitist" revivals in contemporary writings on politics.[13]

By contrast, the aristocratic notion of legitimacy is based on the belief that the capacity to rule is hereditary, and on the disbelief in the capacity of most men to make a sensible choice between different candidates for public office. The same disbelief animates the plutocratic idea of legitimacy, but it argues positively that the acquisition and possession of wealth makes

---

[12] Cf. *Man and His Government*, pp. 239 ff.

[13] Cf. *Man and His Government*, Chapter 18.

for sound rule. We omit here reference to other types of legitimacy and content ourselves with these three kinds of juristic philosophical legitimacy in order to show how the idea of justice intrudes itself into the arguments about legitimacy. It is a special sort of distributive justice, if you will, to assign offices according to merit, variously defined. Though rulership is a burden as well as a prize, let alone a reward,, notions about merit are at work in determining the ground upon which legitimacy is based in a particular community.

But is this all that can be said? Does the problem have to be left in this strictly relative frame of reference? Is there no reason for preferring one kind of legitimacy to another on generally valid grounds? The answer to this question turns upon an aspect of justice that has only recently received a certain amount of attention, and that is the relation of justice to truth.[14]

As with authority, arguments concerning legitimacy cannot be stated without facing the question as to whether the propositions upon which such statements rest are true or not. What is true is admittedly an open question; but the avoidance of claims to absolute truth does not prevent one from recognizing that some statements are more true than others, as far as we know. This possibility affects all statements concerning legitimacy. They, too, are matters of degree. One kind of government, one kind of ruler, is more legitimate than another, and this demonstrable fact profoundly affects the authority and power he is able to wield. This means, however, in its application to legitimacy, that the findings of political science, as well as of of other social sciences, are crucially relevant to a final proposition concerning legitimacy. We have used the term legitimacy to denote whether a given rulership is believed to be based on a good title by most of those subject to it. As scientific knowledge spreads, certain grounds appear to an increasing number of persons no longer right, because the assertions associated with the particular ground are no longer believable; they appear untrue. Quite a few of the types of legitimacy that have played a great role in the past have ceased to do so because scientific knowledge does not permit, for example, the belief in the importance of "blood."

Therefore we can say that legitimacy, being a special case of distributive justice, is affected by the progress of scientific knowledge as it affects the beliefs that can be entertained in any modern community. The weakness of monarchy today is a striking instance of the truth of this propostion. But we must hasten to add that the ideological abuse of scientific knowledge, as it has occurred in modern totalitarian movements, demonstrates the dangers inherent in this relation among science, truth, justice, and legitimacy. For on such ideological abuses of economic and biological knowledge

[14] Cf. *Man and His Government*, Chapter 14.

has been erected the positive claim to legitimacy of communist and fascist rulers. Negatively, these rulers have challenged the claim to legitimacy by democratic rulers, pointing to perversions of the vote by class-motivated capitalists, and in the process undermining the legitimacy of any political order but their own.

At times it has been asserted that not only what is believed by those subject to a particular ruler or regime but also the opinion of the rulers is part of legitimacy. "Legitimacy," Sternberger wrote, "is the foundation of such governmental power as is exercised both with a consciousness on the government's part that it has a right to govern and with some recognition by the governed of that right." I doubt the appropriateness of such inclusion of the belief of the rulers, especially in relating legitimacy to constitutionalism. It would mean that the belief of some constitution-makers that they have a right to do so could legitimize their activity. But it is precisely their capacity to convince others of their right that constitutes the crucial feature of legitimacy. Legitimacy is not a "foundation" of government which is provided in fact by effective power, e.g., military force, but that addition to such brute force which the belief in its rightfulness provides. The often pitiful efforts of new governments to make a constitution are motivated by the belief that such a constitution, if popularly approved, would give them the right to rule, over and above the mere power to do so. Constitutionalism is the modern and secular legitimation of government, prior to any legitimation by performance. In closeknit communities with a strong convictional basis, such as Israel, such legitimation may be dispensed with, and the constitution can then be allowed to "grow" through custom and use.

THE INTERPRETATION OF A CONSTITUTION

OF A

CONSTITUTION

JUDGE

VERSUS

LEGISLATOR

10

A concluding chapter traditionally should offer a summary of the arguments and indicate, if possible, future prospects. In human institutions such as constitutionalism, such a forecast is typically affected by evolving beliefs and hopes of the men composing such institutions. We have had occasion at various points to refer to the beliefs upon which constitutional decisions have been based, at the start and in the course of the evolution of constitutionalism. Constitutionalism, understood as the belief in the basic features of a constitution, such as human dignity and the rights implied in it, and the lust for power and the need for restraining it, is a central feature of Western civilization and its Judaeo-Christian belief system. It might disintegrate and pass away, if that belief system were to die.

Let me recall that in my view constitutionalism in the distinct modern sense did not exist in the world of classical Greece and Rome. Some authorities stress another aspect than the one we have insisted upon, namely that it is believed that man, in his dignity, possesses a sphere that is entirely his own, his "private" sphere which no government nor anyone else has a right to interfere with, and furthermore that in view of the lust of the powerful to do just this, there must be erected barriers—restraints which will keep the powerful out of this private sphere and within the boundaries of those functions assigned to them for the governing of the community.

This conception was alien to the Classics, notably Plato and Aristotle; for not the individual, but the city, the collectivity, was the prime given. Other authorities have stressed "the contrast between the new conception of the conscious formulation by the people of its fundamental law, and the older traditional view in which the word was applied only to substantive principles to be deduced from a nation's actual institutions and their development." [1] Leaving aside the anachronistic use of the term "nation" in this

[1] Charles Howard McIlwain, *Constitutionalism: Ancient and Modern*, 1940, p. 5.

statement, the popular source of a political order is *not* the criterion of what is typically *modern* in constitutionalism.

It is a view which has been revived by the totalitarians in our time. The Soviet Union, in fashioning their constitution in 1919, stressed precisely this popular origin, but failed to provide a division of powers which might protect the individual against the arbitrary power of the party and government. Plato, in *The Statesman,* and following him Aristotle, stressed the popular basis of a *politeia,* usually translated as constitution, as have many others, especially since the sixteenth century.[2] It was an essential precondition to that doctrine of Parliament's omnipotence against which (and not against King George) the Americans revolted, for they rightly claimed to be part of the people.

It has been thoughtfully argued that this doctrine "could never have persisted . . . in England if its edge had not been blunted by conventions. . . ."[3] That is the reason one can speak of the British political order as constitutional; more particularly, the recognition of the opposition as an essential part of that order "divides" the power and protects the individual.[4] The Roman political order with its division into consuls, senate, popular assembly, and the rest has in parallel usually been seen as a constitutional order, but mistakenly so. For this division was not meant to protect the individual, but to provide stability. Certain features of the Roman order, particularly the right of the Roman citizen to be tried according to a particular procedure (made familiar to many by St. Paul's protest against the arbitrary procedure of Festus and his soldiers,[5] have been placed in analogy to *Habeas Corpus* and other modern constitutional principles, but these Roman legal principles were not meant to prevent the government from invading man's private sphere. Rather they were meant to stabilize the legal order, and hence strengthen the Roman Republic.

Yet the Romans did distrust power and those who wielded it. Indeed the institution of two consuls, that is to say, the splitting of the chief executive—never to my knowledge followed elsewhere in the West—was according to Roman legend due to their desire to avoid the repetition of the tyranny of Tarquinius, their last monarch. Again, we find in studying these legends that the *motif* for such division was the quality of the government rather

---

[2] McIlwain, *Constitutionalism,* p. 5; Johannes Althusius (1563–1638) was one of the first who developed a theory of constitutionalism in his *Politica Methodice Digesta* (1603 and later); it has often been misinterpreted as "democracy." See the introduciton to my edition, 1932 (new version—German—1974).

[3] McIlwain, *Constitutionalism,* p. 20.

[4] My *Constitutional Government and Democracy,* 1968b, pp. 178–89, gives further detail.

[5] *Acts,* Chapters 22–26.

than the protection of the individual, as was the entire elaborate Roman system of divided functions, and especially that of the legislative power.

James Harrington, the ardent constitutionalist, when coining his famous formula of the commonwealth as "consisting of the senate proposing, the people resolving, and the magistracy executing," [6] started to shift the ground. John Locke completed this modernization: for him the individual's freedom, and hence the protection of his private sphere, have become the focal point of the matter.[7]

The rapid decline in the interest and belief in such a private sphere and the preoccupation with communal living and many related trends suggest that the future of modern constitutionalism is by no means assured. The hoped-for transformation of totalitarian regimes, notably the Soviet Union, is seen in certain marked recent trends, such as the opposition, primarily intellectual, in the Soviet Union. What a man like Sakharov is demanding is a certain amount of constitutional protection for writers and scientists. Such men oppose censorship and make it a central issue in their ideological struggle.[8] They demand freedom and add the utilitarian argument that the Soviet Union will benefit from such a grant of freedom. It is unfortunate that often in the West the issues involved are misstated and misunderstood. It is not to be seen as a demand for "democracy"; for the Soviet Union understands itself as a democracy, indeed as a better democracy than those found in the West.[9] The issue is that of constitutionalism and of the rule of law. It is the issue of restraining the exercise of arbitrary power by the party and the government.[10]

The decisive institutional question in this connection is the independence of the judiciary. The recognition of the judicial power was the last of the three powers in the evolution of Western constitutionalism. Even in

---

[6] The formula is from *Oceana* (in the Toland edition), pp. 29–31. Cf. also Charles Blitzer's searching study, *An Immortal Commonwealth*, 1960.

[7] See the *Oxford Dictionary* on the early history of the word which acquired its modern meaning in seventeenth-century England. For Locke, cf. M. Seliger, *The Liberal Politics of John Locke*, 1969, especially pp. 322 ff.

[8] Andrei Sakharov, as translated by *The New York Times* under the title *Progress, Coexistence and Intellectual Freedom*, with an introduction, afterword, and notes by Harrison Salisbury, 1968. In his statement, Solzhenitsyn claimed that censorship was illegal and unconstitutional. Sakharov founded a Committee for Human Rights in 1970, and has recently put forward a memorandum (1972, but written the previous year) in which general questions of human rights and public policy are raised; cf. for the text *Die Zeit*, July 25, 1972, p. 3.

[9] Stalin's speech of February 6, 1946, stated this position with great clarity and emphasis. Soviet scholars and writers like Tschikvadze writing on democratic government have made this argument one of the key points of their analysis.

[10] See my, with Michael Curtis and Benjamin R. Barber, *Totalitarianism in Perspective*, 1969, and, with Z. Brzezinski, *Totalitarian Dictatorship and Autocracy*, rev. ed., 1965, Chapter 10.

Britain it was only in 1701, and after the long revolutionary struggle, that the independence of the judiciary was acknowledged in the famous rule that judges shall serve as long as they conduct themselves well (*quamdiu se bene gesserint*). Even in Locke's basic theory the judges had been seen as merely a part of the executive power, the reason being that they constituted part of the law enforcement machinery.

This failure to identify the judicial powers probably resulted from the fact that this power had been the core of royal government in the earlier Middle Ages. For the king was then above all the source of judgments by which what is right was announced. King Louis of France, eventually sainted, was pictured as sitting under an oak tree and judging the men in dispute. The settling of disputes is the primordial function of a political order.[11] Such judging is meant to establish "justice." The maintenance of justice is closely related to the task of maintaining internal peace.

In the course of time, and as the king became a party to many disputes, the monarch was no longer able to fulfill the role of a detached judge. Hence the demand crystallized for having the judges be independent. It was one of the key points of conflict between parliament and the king which the ancient formula of "the king in parliament" had tried to hide. The king in parliament became the king against parliament.

The idea of constitutionalism in the modern key was born when the demand for an independent judiciary arose. A constitution embodies a system of power relationships which have become institutionalized. It is a particular kind of law and as such consists of enforced rules. But it is a living system, dynamic and ever-changing. Thus, a constitutional system changes, but only within the rules involved in its constituent parts. When one of these parts is destroyed, the system perishes with it. For example, federalism in America may undergo important changes, as it has since 1787 and even quite recently; but without any kind of federalism, the American constitutional system would have to be considered replaced by a new and different one. The same might be said of the president and the Congress or of a set of independent courts headed by a supreme court. Systems are known and identified, as we concluded in Chapter 1, through institutional analysis.

Ultimately, we saw that constitutionalism is rooted in certain basic beliefs, the belief in the dignity of man and the belief in man's inclination to abuse power. These beliefs rest upon religious convictions. They require that power be restrained and limited, because power cannot be trusted. Constitutionalism by dividing power provides a system of effective restraints upon governmental action.

Modern constitutionalism is a very particular way of distributing political power by organizing its division. But the customary view of it has

[11] See my *Man and His Government*, 1963b, Chapter 24.

been shown to be based upon too one-sided a view of power. A sounder conception of power, political power, recognizes its dual nature. It is not only a substance that one can possess, but also a relationship which in fact is more basic. Beneath all the divided powers there is found the common power of the community. It feeds, so to speak, the fountains of different powers, such as the legislative, the executive, and the judicial which manifest the power of the community. Power can be understood only as the projection, the manifestation of a community's very existence.

If constitutionalism were an attempt to deny the popular source of power, it would be an empty formal structure. Actually, it is a particular way of structuring this communal power. Such structuring by protecting the private sphere of each individual member of the community serves freedom as a basic value, that is to say, the power of each individual to shape his own life according to his own convictions and preferences. Freedom—or liberty—as the key value is closely linked to constitutionalism.

People among whom liberty is not highly valued will not have much interest in making constitutionalism work. It may not be a mere facade, as some have argued, but it will lack the vitality that alone can assure its continued development and growth. For this reason, constitutionalism is intertwined with the ideologies of liberalism, individualism, and rationalism. Thus freedom of the individual becomes compatible with the freedom of all—under law! Its exercise, we showed, presupposes effective institutions; for these provide the restraints without which power—the power of the individual, as well as that of the group and of the state—is likely to be abused.

In his *On Liberty,* John Stuart Mill wrote that "the only purpose for which power can be rightfully exercised over any member of a civilized community against his will is to prevent harm to others." Only an effective constitution can assure that. It is at this point that the problem of the limiting of democracy presents itself.

Democratic constitutionalism, that is to say, constitutional democracy, is the battle-cry of modern government. Popular democracy is urged as a rival. What the majority of the people want is claimed to be decisive in determining public policy, law, and administration. Majority rule is indeed the quintessence of democracy. But does it mean the "majority-of-one"? De Tocqueville stressed the danger of majority tyranny, and his analysis was echoed in many writings on democracy. The argument stressed the failure of popular democracy to remember constitutionalism and its fear of the abuse of power. But if the majority is limited, it does not conflict with constitutionalism and its apprehension of power. Constitutionalism, when understood as limiting the exercise of power and rule, limits the power of the people as of any other group. Even though the people are the source of all power in the last analysis, in adopting a constitution they limit their own power.

Such auto-limitation is hard to maintain and at times it breaks down. For since a change in the limits imposed upon themselves by a "sovereign" people may constitute a revolution, a democratic constitution has revolutionary potentials built into it. Yet, these potentials exclude violence. Alterations adopted by a majority vote are themselves limited; they substitute ballots for bullets, as the saying goes. "No majority, unless it abrogates democracy, can decide to kill the members of a minority"—and it rarely will want to, we might add. The process of protecting the minority in its opposition to the majority is inherent in the concept of constitutional majority rule itself.[12]

Such minority protection is often accomplished by a federal constitution. Modern constitutionalism having arisen in conjunction with contractual theories of government, as exemplified by John Locke, it was logical to see a federal union as an agreement between divergent territorially defined groups. Thus, modern federalism became a corollary of modern constitutionalism. Federalism in a sense is a constitutionally guaranteed decentralization and is hence difficult to distinguish from a constitutionally protected local self-government such as has been traditional in England.

A federal constitution has another central function besides protecting local autonomy; for it also separates powers. Like the functional division of powers, it organizes a more or less effective restraint upon the abuse or misuse of governmental power, not only by the central, but by the local governments as well. In quite a few situations, such territorial division of power has proved more effective than the functional one. What federalism does is to mobilize firmly entrenched local powers in support of the constitution, by offering them protection.

Federal constitutionalism shares with all constitutionalism the problems of adjusting a relatively rigid structure to the changing exigencies of modern industrialism. Under its conditions friction and conflict are likely to develop whenever technological change radically transforms social life. More especially, new functions challenge the established distribution of competencies, as, e.g., in road-building and communications, and more than ever in the provision of welfare services. In the absence of constitutional provisions, new patterns of cooperation emerge which eventually call for institutionalization. In the discussion in America over constitutional reform, the federal system plays a central role; the existing system is markedly

---

[12] Hellmut Wollman, *Die Stellung der parlamentarischen Minderheiten in England, der Bundesrepublik Deutschland und Italien*, 1970.

antiquated. Responding to new demands and changing patterns of relations between central and local governments will require constitutional amendments in many western countries, especially in federalism.

The value of federalism as a method for protecting minorities has, of course, been marked in the field of human rights. As we have seen, such rights are very central to constitutionalism. Once thought of as unchangeable (natural) rights, they are now recognized as something changing in time and place. Their source is not some kind of natural law, but the values cherished by a particular community. It is, to use a conventional phrase, the popular will, as expressed in a constitution. Such rights are political in the sense of emerging from the political process, and hence alterable in response to it.

Rights have come to be seen as liberties and freedoms. Under a constitution, they are often described as "inviolable" and "inalienable," though if they were inviolable in any strict sense, no constitutional protection would be needed. The term "inviolable" is evidently meant normatively, and means to say that "they may not be violated." Moreover, the *reservatio mentalis* remains that a right (liberty, freedom) may be altered by constitutional amendment. Thus, human rights express and make explicit the basic values; many of them are shared by most of mankind as expressed in the *Universal Declaration of Human Rights*, adopted by the United Nations.

Hence we may conclude that no legal document that calls itself a constitution may be said to be genuine if it lacks a guarantee of specified human rights and provisions for their enforcement. Hence the Americans who were inclined to reject the Constitution in 1787 unless assured that Congress would at once add a bill of rights were fundamentally right, and what they added has been seen as part of the original document.

But a serious problem remains: what is to be done when the survival of the constitutional order is threatened by the abuse of these rights? Should they be denied or suspended? It is the problem of constitutional crisis and emergency, that is to say, of constitutional reason of state. War apart, constitutional reason of state calls for a recognition of the danger inherent in constitutionalism. Thus in the last analysis, there are limits to the realization of freedom. Yet, constitutionalism stands and falls with the protection of human dignity, the most fundamental basis of which is the right of a man to his conviction, his belief, his faith. To make a man's innermost self secure is more crucial to the security and survival of a constitutional order than any secret.

It is thus the very core of constitutional reason of state, for it is the reason why a constitutional state is founded and maintained. Laws like the British Public Order Act of 1936, adopted to cope with Nazi sympathizers and their activities, are commendable, because this Act concentrates upon actual observable behavior, rather than opinions or beliefs. The same cannot, unfortunately, be said of laws adopted in the United States and elsewhere. In particular, vaguely worded criminal laws against something called "conspiracy" constitute threats to constitutional freedoms. The defects of this approach were shown to lead to the conclusion that it is most undesirable to leave this problem to administrative discretion.

Administrative discretion and more especially how to delimit it are of basic concern to constitutionalism and its theory. For the very legitimacy of constitutionalism is here involved. Many of those who think that they can legitimize their rule by adopting a constitution overlook this vital question. For a constitution that leaves administrative discretion undefined, or even partially open, fails to provide such legitimation. Even partial infractions, on the plea of necessity (according to Milton's great phrase, "the tyrant's plea") call for vigorous remedial action. The same thing may be said for many questionable executive or administrative acts committed in the name of "national security."

Legitimacy is not, as we saw, the "foundation" of government, for in fact government is founded upon effective force. It is an addition, founded upon the belief that such force is rightfully exercised. Constitutionalism is capable of generating such a belief which may be reinforced by good performance. Not the king as symbol of a sacred deity, but a constitution as the symbol of hallowed tradition provides the needed evidence that the actual ruler has a right to rule.

Such a constitution, in its role as a symbol, would seem to be unalterable, must be unalterable! And yet, it was recognized from the outset that a constitution to be lasting must be adapted and interpreted to adjust it to changing circumstances. "Half seeing this in the mists of the future, the Founding Fathers established the Supreme Court. So in many ways the Constitution has been what that Court declared it to be, and necessarily so." [13] Actually, these Fathers also provided a process of amending the constitution, as has been done ever since, though the idea was novel at the end of the eighteenth century. (We should note that at that very time, constitution-makers in France after the Revolution still thought they could fashion a constitution that would last forever. What they fashioned lasted only a few years.)

But the amending process proved much too cumbersome and has produced only a little more than a dozen amendments in the near 200 years since it was adopted. Hence one of the great judges of this century could, looking back over the Constitution's history, say that "the Constitution is what the judges say it is." He could therefore call the judges "the safeguard of our liberty and of our property."

Europeans, imbued with the doctrine of sovereignty, first monarchical

---

[13] Charles Evans Hughes, *Addresses and Papers*, 1908, pp. 133 ff.

and later popular, have been very reluctant to accept this truth about constitutionalism. Only in this century has the idea of judicial review made significant progress. The Germans, the Italians, and the French have reluctantly and haltingly embraced the idea that a government according to law and subject to it *(Rechtsstaat)* is necessarily a government of judges to a considerable extent, a *Rechterstaat*.[14]

When, in the early fifties, a group of American scholars was asked by a European constituent assembly to advise them on a constitution for Europe, their advice on the judicial power was clothed in these words:

> *The essentials (of a judicial system for a federated Europe) are: an independent judiciary, resting on definite guarantees of tenure and non-diminished compensation and on a fixed method of appointment; and a Supreme Court with the power to declare legislation or executive acts of the federal or state governments to be in conflict with the federal constitution, as well as the power to interpret and apply federal legislation.*[15]

There was bitter controversy among the recipients of this advice, and since the constitution did not come into force, it is idle to speculate what might have happened. What matters to us here is that the judge was recognized as having the decisive voice in interpreting a constitution. And therefore when in popular parlance and in political oratory the CONSTITUTION is cited as an authoritative statement on a given point, what is or ought to be meant is the constitution as interpreted not only by legislators, but by judges, and ultimately particularly by them.

For who can say what the words in a constitution *mean* without consulting the decisions of the courts in which such meaning is explicated and authoritatively circumscribed? [16] The paradox that the constitution may mean different propositions at different times is inherent in its very nature. It seeks to state in general and hence in abstract terms how the government and the citizens are expected to behave and usually do behave.

---

[14] René Marcic, *Vom Gesetzesstaat zum Richterstaat*, 1957.

[15] Paul Freund in his contribution on the judiciary in *Studies in Federalism*, ed. R. R. Bowie and Carl J. Friedrich, 1954, p. 122.

[16] On this, see basically the work by C. K. Ogden and I. A. Richards, *The Meaning of Meaning*, 1938.

SELECTED BIBLIOGRAPHY

ADLER, MORTIMER. 1958. *The Idea of Freedom*, Vol. I. New York: Doubleday.

BACHRACH, PETER, and MORTON BARATZ. 1970. *Power and Poverty: Theory and Practice.* New York: Oxford University Press.

BAILYN, BERNARD. 1967. *The Ideological Origins of the American Revolution.* Cambridge: Harvard University Press.

BALDWIN, JAMES. 1961. *Nobody Knows My Name.* New York: Dial Press.

BAY, CHRISTIAN. 1958. *The Structure of Freedom.* Stanford: Stanford University Press.

BECKER, CARL. 1942. *The Declaration of Independence.* New York: Knopf.

BERLIN, ISAIAH. 1958. *Two Concepts of Liberty.* New York: Oxford University Press. (Also published in *Four Essays on Liberty*, pp. 118–72. New York: Oxford University Press, 1968.)

BLITZER, CHARLES. 1960. *An Immortal Commonwealth: Political Thought of James Harrington.* New Haven: Yale University Press.

BOTERO, GIOVANNI. 1956. *Reason of State*, trans. P. J. and D. P. Waley. New Haven: Yale University Press.

BOWIE, ROBERT R., and CARL J. FRIEDRICH, eds. 1954. *Studies in Federalism.* Boston: Little, Brown.

BRAUNTHAL, GERHARD. 1962. "Federalism in Germany: The Broadcasting Controversy," *Journal of Politics*, 24: 560–61.

BUCK, PAUL H. 1937. *Road to Reunion, 1865–1900.* Boston: Little, Brown.

BURNHAM, JAMES. 1943. *The Machiavellians: Defenders of Freedom.* New York: John Day Co.

BUTTERIELD, H. 1949. *Christianity and History.* New York: Scribner's.

CAHN, EDMOND N., ed. 1963. *The Great Rights.* New York: Macmillan.

CARDOZO, BENJAMIN N. 1921. *The Nature of the Judicial Process.* New Haven: Yale University Press.

CHAFEE, ZECHARIAH, JR. 1952. *How Human Rights Got into the Constitution.* Boston: Boston University Press.

———. 1956. *Three Human Rights in the Constitution of 1787.* Lawrence: The University Press of Kansas.

CHAPMAN, JOHN W. 1956. *Rousseau: Totalitarian or Liberal?* New York: Columbia University Press.

CLAUDE, INIS L. 1959. *Swords into Plowshares*, rev. ed. New York: Random House.

COLE, TAYLOR. 1958. "The West German Federal Constitutional Court: An Evaluation After Six Years," *Journal of Politics*, 20: 278 ff.

———. 1966. "New Dimensions of West German Federalism," *Comparative Politics and Political Theory*: 99–122.

CRANSTON, MAURICE. 1963. *What Are Human Rights?* New York: Basic Books.

DAHL, ROBERT A. 1956. *A Preface to Democratic Theory*. Chicago: University of Chicago Press.

———, ed. 1966. *Political Oppositions in Western Democracies*. New Haven: Yale University Press.

DE GRAZIA, SEBASTIAN. 1948. *The Political Community: Study of Anomie*. Chicago: University of Chicago Press.

"Democracy and Education in the Current Crisis," *Teachers College Record* (November 1940): 101 ff.

DIETZE, GOTTFRIED. 1958. "America and Europe—Decline and Emergence of Judicial Review," *Virginia Law Review*, 44: 1233 ff.

———. 1963. *In Defense of Property*. Chicago: Henry Regnery.

DODGE, GUY H., ed. 1971. *Jean-Jacques Rousseau: Authoritarian Libertarian?* Problems in Political Science Series. Lexington, Mass.: Heath.

ELLIOT, WILLIAM Y. 1935. *The Need for Constitutional Reform*. New York: McGraw-Hill.

EZERA, KALU. 1960. *Constitutional Developments in Nigeria*. New York: Cambridge University Press.

FAINSOD, MERLE. 1963. *How Russia Is Ruled*, rev. ed. Cambridge: Harvard University Press.

FAST, HOWARD. 1969. *Freedom Road*. New York: Crown Publishers.

FERRERO, G. 1942. *The Principles of Power*. New York: Putnam's.

FRANKFURTER, FELIX, and JAMES M. LANDIS. 1928. *The Business of the Supreme Court—A Study in the Federal Judicial System*. New York: Macmillan.

FRAZIER, J. G. 1959. *The New Golden Bough*, ed. T. H. Gaster. New York: Doubleday.

FREUND, PAUL A. 1955. "Umpiring the Federal System." In Arthur MacMahon, ed., *Federalism: Mature and Emergent*. New York: Doubleday.

FRIEDRICH, CARL J. 1925. "Origin and Development of the Concept of Federalism in the United States," *Jahrbuch des öffentlichen Rechts der Gegenwart*, Neue Folge, Band 9: 29 ff.

———. 1932. *Constitutional Government and Politics*. New York: Harper & Row.

———. 1941. *The New Belief in the Common Man*. Boston: Little Brown. Updated as *Die Demokratie als Herrschaftund Lebensform*, 2nd ed. (1966).

———. 1942. "Rights, Liberties, Freedoms," *University of Pennsylvania Law Review*, 91: 321 ff.

———. 1948. *Inevitable Peace*. Cambridge: Harvard University Press. (Reprinted in 1970 by Greenwood Press, Westport, Conn.)

———. 1950. *The New Image of the Common Man*, 2nd ed. Boston: Beacon Press.

———, ed. 1953. *The Philosophy of Georg W. Hegel*. New York: Modern Library, Inc.

———. 1955. "The Political Thought of Neoliberalism," *American Political Science Review*, 49: 509 ff.

————. 1957. *Constitutional Reason of State: The Survival of the Constitutional Order.* Providence, R. I.: Brown University Press.

————. 1959. "The New French Constitution in Political and Historical Perspective," *Harvard Law Review,* 72: 801 ff.

————. 1963a. "Federalism, National and International in Theory and Practice." Paper read before the Oxford Round Table Meeting of the International Political Science Association in 1963.

————. 1963b. *Man and His Government.* New York: McGraw-Hill.

————. 1963c. *The Philosophy of Law in Historical Perspective,* 2nd ed. Chicago: University of Chicago Press.

————. 1964. *Transcendant Justice—The Religious Dimension of Constitutionalism.* Durham, N.C.: Duke University Press.

————. 1967. *The Impact of American Constitutionalism Abroad.* Boston: Boston University Press.

————. 1968a. *Constitutional Government and Democracy,* 4th ed. Waltham, Mass.: Blaisdell Publishing Co.

————. 1968b. *Trends of Federalism in Theory and Practice.* New York: Praeger.

————. 1970. "Bureaucracy Faces Anarchy." *Canadian Public Administration,* 13: 219-31.

————. 1972. *Tradition and Authority.* London: Pall Mall.

————, and Z. BRZEZINSKI. 1967. *Totalitarian Dictatorship and Autocracy,* 2nd rev. ed. New York: Praeger.

FRIEDRICH, CARL J., and TAYLOR COLE. 1932. *Responsible Bureaucracy—A Study of the Swiss Civil Service.* (Reprinted in 1967 by Russell & Russell Publishers.)

————, MICHAEL CURTIS, and BENJAMIN R. BARBER. 1969. *Totalitarianism in Perspective: Three Views.* New York: Praeger.

————, and ROBERT G. McCLOSKEY. 1954. *From the Declaration of Independence to the Constitution.* Indianapolis: Bobbs-Merrill.

FROMM, ERICH. 1941. *Escape from Freedom.* New York: Holt, Rinehart & Winston.

GARDINER, SAMUEL R. 1906. *Constitutional Documents of the Puritan Revolution,* 3rd ed. Oxford: Clarendon Press.

GARDNER, GEORGE K. 1936. "The Constitutional Questions Raised by the Flag Salute and the Teachers' Oath Acts in Massachusetts," *Boston University Law Review,* 16: 803 ff.

GOUGH, J. W. 1950. *John Locke's Political Philosophy.* New York: Oxford University Press.

GREAVES, H. R. G. 1955. *The British Constitution,* 3rd ed. New York: Cambridge University Press.

HAVELOCK, ERIC A. 1957. *The Liberal Temper in Greek Politics.* New Haven: Yale University Press.

HAZLITT, HENRY. 1942. *A New Constitution Now.* New York: McGraw-Hill.

HECHSCHER, ELI F. 1935. *Mercantilism,* 2 vols. New York: Macmillan.

HOFSTADTER, RICHARD, and WALTER P. METZGER. 1955. *The Development of Academic Freedom in the United States.* New York: Columbia University Press.

HOLCOMBE, A. H. 1948. *Human Rights in the Modern World.* New York: New York Univerity Press.

HYNEMAN, CHARLES. 1950. *Bureaucracy in a Democracy.* New York: Harper & Row.

KENDALL, WILLMORE. 1939. "The Majority Principle and the Scientific Elite," *Southern Review*, 4 (Winter): 463.

———. 1941. *John Locke and the Doctrine of Majority-Rule*. Illinois Studies in the Social Sciences, Vol. 26, No. 2. Urbana: University of Illinois Press.

KEY, V. O., JR. 1949. *Southern Politics*. New York: Knopf.

KIRK, RUSSELL. 1955. *Academic Freedom—An Essay in Definition*. Chicago: Regnery.

KORNHAUSER, WILLIAM. 1959. *The Politics of Mass Society*. New York: Free Press.

KROEBER, A. L. 1948. *Anthropology*, rev. ed. New York: Harcourt.

KUHN HELMUT. 1970. *Jugend im Aufbruch*. Munich: Koesel.

LASSWELL HAROLD D., and ABRAHAM KAPLAN. 1950. *Power and Society*. New Haven: Yale University Press.

LAUTERPACHT, H. 1951. *International Law and Human Rights*. New York: Praeger.

LERNER, MAX. 1938. "Minority Rule and the Constitutional Tradition." In C. Read, *The Constitution Reconsidered*. New York: Columbia University Press.

LINDSAY, A. D. 1943. *The Modern Democratic State*, 1st American ed., vol. 1. Royal Institute of International Affairs. New York: Oxford University Press.

LIPPINCOTT, BENJAMIN. 1938. *Victorian Critics of Democracy*. Minneapolis: University of Minnesota Press.

LIPSET, SEYMOUR MARTIN. 1959. *Political Man: The Social Bases of Politics*. New York: Doubleday.

LLWELLYN, RICHARD. 1961. *A Man in a Mirror*. New York: Pocket Books.

LOWENSTEIN, KARL. 1940. *Hitler's Germany: The Nazi Background to War*, rev. ed. New York: Macmillan.

———. 1946. *Political Reconstruction*. New York: Macmillan.

———. 1957. *Political Power and the Governmental Process*. Chicago: University of Chicago Press.

———. 1967. *British Cabinet Government*. New York: Oxford University Press.

MAASS, ARTHUR, ed. 1959. *Area and Power*. New York: Free Press.

McBAIN, HOWARD LEE. 1929. *The Living Constitution: A Constitution of the Realities and the Legends of Our Fundamental Law*. World To-day Bookshelf. New York: Macmillan.

McCLOSKEY, ROBERT G. 1960. *The American Supreme Court*. Chicago: University of Chicago Press.

———. 1962. "Economic Due Process and the Supreme Court: An Exhumation and Re-burial," *The Supreme Court Review*: 62 ff.

McILWAIN, CHARLES H. 1910. *The High Court of Parliament and Its Supremacy*. New Haven: Yale University Press.

———. 1938. "The Fundamental Law Behind the Constitution of the United States." In C. Read, ed., *The Constitution Reconsidered*. New York: Columbia University Press.

———. 1940. *Constitutionalism: Ancient and Modern*. Ithaca, N.Y.: Cornell University Press.

McIVER, ROBERT M. 1955. *Academic Freedom in Our Time*. New York: Columbia University Press.

MacMAHON, ARTHUR W. 1955. *Federalism: Mature and Emergent*. New York: Doubleday.

McWHINNEY, EDWARD. 1962a. *Comparative Federalism—States' Rights and National Power*. Toronto: University of Toronto Press.

————. 1962b. *Constitutionalism in Germany and the Federal Constitutional Court.* New York: Oceana.

MAIR, LUCY. 1963. *Primitive Government.* New York: Penguin.

MARSHALL, BURKE. 1964. *Federalism and Civil Rights.* New York: Columbia University Press.

MEGILL, KENNETH A. 1970. *The New Democratic Theory.* New York: Free Press.

MEINECKE, FRIEDRICH. 1965. *Machiavellism: The Doctrine of Raison d'Etat and Its Place in Modern History,* trans. D. Scott. New York: Praeger.

MERRIAM, CHARLES E. 1936. *Power.* New York: Viking.

MERTON, R. K., ed. 1952. *Reader in Bureaucracy.* New York: Free Press.

MILLETT, JOHN. 1959. *Government and Public Administration: The Quest for Responsible Performance.* New York: McGraw-Hill.

MORRIS-JONES, W. H. 1965. "On Constitutionalism," *American Political Science Review,* 59: 439 ff.

MORROW, GLENN R. 1968. "Academic Freedom." In *International Encyclopedia of the Social Sciences,* Vol. 1.

MYERS, D. P. 1956. "The European Commission on Human Rights," *American Journal of International Law,* 50.

MYRDAL, GUNNAR, with RICHARD STERNER and ARNOLD ROSE. 1944. *An American Dilemma.* New York: Harper.

NEUMANN, FRANZ L. 1955. "Federalism and Freedom: A Critique." In Arthur W. MacMahon, ed., *Federalism: Mature and Emergent.* New York: Doubleday.

NIEBUHR, REINHOLD. 1940. *Christianity and Power Politics.* New York: Scribner's.

ORLINSKY, HARRY M. 1954. *Ancient Israel.* Ithaca, N.Y.: Cornell University Press.

PARSONS, TALCOTT. 1950. *The Social System.* New York: Free Press.

PELTASON, JACK W. 1961. *Fifty-eight Lonely Men.* New York: Harcourt.

POCOCK, J. G. A. 1947. *The Ancient Constitution and the Feudal Law.* New York: Cambridge University Press.

PROTHERO, G. W., ed. 1913. *Select Statutes and Other Constitutional Documents Illustrative of the Reigns of Elizabeth and James I,* 4th ed. New York: Oxford University Press.

READ, C., ed. 1938. *The Constitution Reconsidered.* New York: Columbia University Press.

REICH, DONALD R. 1963. "Court, Comity, and Federalism in West Germany," *Midwest Journal of Political Science,* 7: 197–228.

ROSSITER, C. L. 1948. *Constitutional Dictatorship.* Princeton: Princeton University Press.

*Royal Commission on the Constitution. 1969-1973. Volume I: *Report.* Volume II: *Memorandum of Dissent.* London: October 1973.

RUSSELL, BERTRAND. 1938. *Power.* New York: Viking.

SABINE, GEORGE H. 1954. *A History of Political Theory,* rev. ed. New York: Henry Holt.

SAFRAN, NADAV. 1963. *The United States and Israel.* Cambridge: Harvard University Press.

SAKAROV, ANDREI. 1968. *Progress, Coexistence and Intellectual Freedom,* trans. *The New York Times,* with introduction and notes by Harrison Salisbury. New York: Norton C. Norton.

* This important report only appeared after completion of this manuscript.

SARTORI, GIOVANNI. 1962a. "Constitutionalism: A Preliminary Discussion," *American Political Science Review*, 56: 853–65.

———. 1962b. *Democratic Theory*. Detroit: Wayne State University Press.

SCHOENBAUM, DAVID. 1968. *The Spiegel Affair*. New York: Doubleday.

SELIGER, M. 1969. *The Liberal Politics of John Locke*. New York: Praeger.

SENATE COMMITTEE ON GOVERNMENT OPERATIONS. 1963. *Intergovernmental Operations*, Report No. 84, 88th Congress. Washington, D.C.: Government Printing Office.

SENATE SUBCOMMITTEE ON REORGANIZATION OF THE COMMITTEE ON GOVERNMENT OPERATIONS. 1955. *Commission on Government Security*, 84th Congress. Washington, D.C.: Government Printing Office.

SHKLAR, JUDITH N. 1969. *Men and Citizens*. New York: Cambridge University Press.

SKILLING, H. GORDON, and FRANKLIN GRIFFITHS, eds. 1970. *Interest Groups in Soviet Politics*. Princeton: Princeton University Press.

SMELLIE, K. B. 1962. *Great Britain Since 1688*. Ann Arbor: University of Michigan Press.

SMITH, PAGE. 1962. *John Adams*. 2 vols. New York: Doubleday.

SPIRO, HERBERT. 1969. *Responsibility in Government: Theory and Practice*. New Perspectives in Political Science Series. New York: Van Nostrand-Reinhold.

STAHL, O. GLENN. 1971. *Public Personnel Administration*, 6th ed. New York: Harper & Row.

STRONG, C. F. 1963. *A History of Modern Political Constitutions*. New York: Putnam.

SUNDQUIST, R. 1969. *Making Federalism Work*. Washington, D.C.: Brookings Institution.

SUTHERLAND, ARTHUR E. 1965. *Constitutionalism in America—Origin and Evolution of its Fundamental Ideas*. Waltham, Mass.: Blaisdell.

TALMON, J. L. 1952. *The Rise of Totalitarian Democracy*. New York: Beacon Press.

TILMAN, ROBERT O., and TAYLOR COLE, eds. 1962. *The Nigerian Political Scene*. Durham, N.C.: Duke University Press.

TREVES, G., ed. 1969. *Diritto delle Communita Europee e Diritto degli Stati Membri*. Milan; Ferro Edizioni.

TUGWELL, REXFORD G. 1970. *A Model Constitution for a United Republics of America*. Santa Barbara, Calif.: Center for the Study of Democratic Institutions.

ULAM, ADAM. 1968. *Expansion and Coexistence—The History of Soviet Foreign Policy, 1917–1967*. New York: Praeger.

VON BEYME, KLAUS. 1964. "Federal Theory and Party Reality in the Soviet Union," *Public Policy*, 13: 394–412.

WATKINS, FREDERICK M. 1939. *The Failure of Constitutional Emergency Powers under the German Republic*. Harvard Political Studies, number 10. Cambridge: Harvard University Press.

WHEARE, K. C. 1953. *Federal Government*, 3rd ed. New York: Oxford University Press.

WHEELER, HARVEY. 1968. *Democracy in a Revolutionary Era*. New York: Praeger.

WILSON, BRYAN. 1970. *The Youth Culture and the Universities*. London: Faber & Faber.

WILSON, JAMES Q. 1963. "The Police and Their Problems: A Theory," *Public Policy*, 12: 189 ff.

WILSON, O. W. 1950. *Police Administration*. New York: McGraw-Hill.

INDEX